NWH

ACPL ITEM
DISCARDED

She Was There
Stories of Pioneering Women Journalists

To work in journalism in the early days was a special challenge for women. But the difficulties they faced seemed to spur them on to try for the most daring jobs. Here are the stories of fifteen important women journalists who worked from the twenties to today, covering everything from crime to war to the White House. From Emma Bugbee who reported on the campaign for votes for women to Marie Torre and Helen Thomas, among others working today, *She Was There* tells a fast-moving story of adventure and unswerving dedication in pursuit of the reporter's trade.

She Was There
Stories of Pioneering Women Journalists

Jean E. Collins

Photographs

JULIAN MESSNER
NEW YORK

ALLEN COUNTY PUBLIC LIBRARY
FORT WAYNE, INDIANA

Copyright © 1980 by Jean E. Collins

All rights reserved including the right of
reproduction in whole or in part in any form.
Published by Julian Messner, a Simon & Schuster
Division of Gulf & Western Corporation,
Simon & Schuster Building,
1230 Avenue of the Americas,
New York, New York 10020.

JULIAN MESSNER and colophon are trademarks of
Simon & Schuster, registered in the U.S. Patent
and Trademark Office.

Manufactured in the United States of America.

Design by Irving Perkins

Library of Congress Cataloging in Publication Data

Collins, Jean E
  She was there.
  Includes index.
  SUMMARY: Fifteen women journalists from the 1920's to today tell in their own words the demands and rewards they experienced in their profession.
  1. Women journalists—United States—Biography—Juvenile literature. [1. Journalists] I. Title.
PN4872.C6   070'.92'2 [B] [920]   80-36769
ISBN 0-671-33082-9

*For Peter Eric Liggett
and Sarah Collins Liggett*

In memory of Maebelle Baker Breen

2119533

Contents

Introduction 11

PART ONE
CHAPTER 1 Emma Bugbee—Votes for Women 21
CHAPTER 2 Kathleen McLaughlin—Covering Chicago Gangsters 27
CHAPTER 3 Eleanor Roosevelt and Her Press Group 34
CHAPTER 4 Mildred Gilman—Stunt Reporter, Sob Sister, and Foreign Correspondent 52
CHAPTER 5 Norma Abrams—Reporting for a Tabloid 67

PART TWO
CHAPTER 6 Sonia Tomara—War Correspondent 77
CHAPTER 7 Irene Corbally Kuhn—Radio Journalist and War Correspondent 85
CHAPTER 8 Carolyn Anspacher—San Francisco Cityside Reporter 93
CHAPTER 9 Hazel Garland—Newspaper Editor 103
CHAPTER 10 Mary Morris—Photojournalist 119

PART THREE
CHAPTER 11 Mary Garber—Sportswriter 131
CHAPTER 12 Judith Crist—Drama and Film Critic ... 142
CHAPTER 13 Celestine Sibley—Atlanta Columnist and Reporter 154
CHAPTER 14 Marie Torre—Freedom of the Press 164
CHAPTER 15 Helen Thomas—White House Bureau Chief 178

Index 187

Acknowledgments

I'm deeply grateful to each woman who shared her life and work experiences with me and with the readers of this book. I treasure the friendships that have developed with some of them. Many of the women went out of their way to make time for interviews, furnish photographs, and to refer me to other journalists. To each one, a hearty thank you for being a part of the book.

I also appreciated the opportunity to work at the Writers Room in New York City, where much of the work on the book was done.

Barnard Alumnae magazine gave permission to exerpt and reprint material that originally appeared in its Winter 1976 issue in an article by the author titled "Two of Barnard's Nellie Blys." *Matrix*, the magazine of Women in Communications, Inc., kindly gave the rights to an article by the author that appeared in the Spring 1976 *Matrix* under the title "Kathleen McLaughlin, Journalist: An Oral History."

Many individuals gave invaluable help of various kinds, and I want to thank each of them here. They include Audrey Adler, John S. Anson, Ann B. Collins, Robert A. Collins, Janice Harayda, John P. Liggett, Maurine D. Liggett, Peter E. Liggett, Melvin Mencher, Iris Rosoff, Jane Steltenpohl, and Blanche Wood.

Introduction

She Was There is about journalists who made history as they reported on history-in-the-making. Fifteen women tell, in their own words, the stories of how they pioneered in a field that was just opening up to women. They describe the glamour, demands, and rewards of this important profession.

Most of the women in *She Was There* are now in their sixties, seventies, and eighties. They were reporters during the era that bridges the two most recent swells of strength in the struggle for women's equality—the suffrage movement, which resulted in women winning the right to vote in 1920, and the current effort to ratify the Equal Rights Amendment. Emma Bugbee, the first journalist you'll read about, reported on the campaign for votes for women. The book closes with a chapter on Helen Thomas, the White House bureau chief for United Press International wire service, who talks about the status of women today.

The women you'll meet here also covered crime, the world wars, Eleanor Roosevelt, Hollywood, sports, and the civil rights movement. They wrote, broadcast, and in one case, photographed it all. Mildren Gilman drank bootleg whiskey while reporting on the speakeasies that served it

INTRODUCTION

in the days of Prohibition, when it was against the law to make and sell liquor. Dorothy Ducas covered a fire on the first day of her honeymoon. Sonia Tomara flew on a bombing mission over Japan during World War II. Norma Abrams ran up a thousand-dollar rental car bill while covering a wedding. Marie Torre went to jail because of her belief in press freedom. Mary Morris leaned out a trapdoor on top of the Empire State Building to take photographs of New York City for the Associated Press.

She Was There had its beginnings in my six-month search for Emma Bugbee. I made about fifteen telephone calls, wrote five letters, and spent several dizzying hours scanning microfilm of the *New York Herald Tribune,* where she worked for fifty-five years. Each lead evaporated until I finally located a former *Herald Tribune* reporter who gave me the name of a nursing home where Emma Bugbee lived at one time. When I received this man's letter, I immediately called the Sunny View Nursing Home in Warwick, Rhode Island, not knowing whether she was even alive, much less at the home. A staff member answered the phone and asked me to "hold the line because it's difficult for her to walk." I was elated to have located her.

When she finally reached the phone, I explained that I had heard about her from a Columbia University journalism professor of mine who had known her years ago when she lived in New York. He had suggested that I interview her about her coverage of Eleanor Roosevelt. Bugbee agreed on an interview date and said she thought it would be fun, "Once we get started."

I rode a bus from New York to Rhode Island several weeks later on a colorful October Saturday. She was sitting

Introduction

in a wheelchair in a pleasant corner room which indeed had a "sunny view" and was decorated with oil canvases she had begun painting after her retirement. An old green eyeshade, the type that copy editors used to wear to protect their eyes from glaring newsroom lights, hung on the wall.

Emma Bugbee reminded me of Eleanor Roosevelt with her tall frame, expressive face, and loosely pulled-back hair. As we talked, she sometimes rolled a word out extra slowly to emphasize her point, as in her remark on newspaper work: "We thought it was *w o n d e r f u l*." We talked about the moving, funny, important moments in her career; her eyes brimmed with tears when she spoke about the day she retired.

Emma Bugbee told me about other women journalists she worked with, and I interviewed some of them. Each women I spoke with seemed to lead to at least one other. At that point, I didn't realize that the interviews would become a book. I just developed a growing sense that these early journalists' recollections, thoughts, and feelings about their work should be preserved. I found what they had to say fascinating, inspiring, and informative and hope that others will too.

The women in *She Was There* are a select group, but there are other distinguished pioneering women journalists still living. And the tradition of women journalists goes back even further, from a handful of widows who took over their husbands' newspapers in colonial days to reporter Nellie Bly who completed her record-breaking seventy-two-day trip around the world in 1890.

The stories presented here are in the first person in order to show the vitality these women still have today and

INTRODUCTION

to make the events they talk about seem as immediate as possible. The book doesn't give all the traditional facts about each woman's life or even about each long and varied career. Instead, I chose episodes that I believe are most important, colorful, or revealing of a quality or experience that is common to many early women journalists. I did find several common threads running through their lives.

Most of them approached their profession single-mindedly, deciding early, sometimes in elementary school, that they wanted to be reporters and never changing their minds. Several women chose to follow their instincts where they led rather than to pursue a single goal. Even so, they eventually focused their activities and skills and put them to good use in journalism, as Carolyn Anspacher did with her training as an actress.

Some of the women started newspapers when they were young girls and circulated them in their neighborhoods. One woman, as a youngster, made twenty-two carbon copies when she typed her newspaper so that she would not have to keep retyping. She explained that by the time someone received the eighth copy, he or she was a little puzzled as to what the paper was about.

Some, although certainly not all, of the women had the advantages of family money, which they used to obtain fine educations and to travel. They had an advantage when it came to gaining entrée to potential employers, but still had to prove themselves on the job.

Most had at least one encouraging, devoted parent, and often an inspiring teacher. Those who married, almost to a one, had husbands who wholeheartedly supported their working. Several of them had children too, even though it was less acceptable then for women to combine family and professional life.

A keen sense of humor helped smooth the way for many of the women. They say they couldn't have survived without the ability to laugh at themselves and their occasional predicaments, whether it was being falsely accused of murder or getting stuck in a deep Japanese bathtub and having to be rescued by the hotel manager.

Self-confidence in job hunting, even pretended confidence, often paid off. Mildred Gilman told an editor that she'd never worked for a newspaper for less than a hundred dollars a week, neglecting to add that she'd never worked for a newspaper at all. She started at the then lofty salary of a hundred dollars when the going rate for men was sixty dollars a week. World War II created new job openings for women, and many got their start in journalism when men reporters were "called to the colors," as Sonia Tomara put it.

Women were discriminated against in many ways, although it usually wasn't considered discrimination several decades ago. What these women believed was their good fortune, some would consider tokenism today. Emma Bugbee said, "Everybody thinks I was high in journalism, but there were eleven newspapers in New York, and they all had at least one woman on the staff." Several women credit the suffragists who preceded them with helping pave the way for their opportunities. Others believe their success was the result of good luck or their own dedication and talent. One explained that it always seemed so simple to her to live her own life that she's "never been able to see what all the shooting's about."

INTRODUCTION

Each woman, nevertheless, had to find ways to overcome obstacles that came with working in a "man's world." When Eva vom Baur became editor of the women's page of the *New York Sun* in 1916, there was no women's bathroom. Someone had to knock a hole in a wall so that the new women staff members at the *Sun* could use the women's bathroom at the newspaper next door.

Hard work and perseverance were as essential as typewriter and paper. The women developed strong, sturdy egos that helped them to cope with discrimination and other difficulties they faced. When they needed help, they usually turned to a more experienced reporter, woman or man, rather than make any united effort.

It was astonishingly common for them to find great joy in their work and to thrive on their adventures. Yet their jobs were not easy. Some assignments were downright dangerous, as when Mildred Gilman descended to the bottom of a New Jersey river one freezing February day wearing an old, patched diving suit and with no means of rescue had she gotten into trouble. But she and other women reporters tackled almost any assignment they were given and found their lives were enriched as a result.

Advancing age has slowed a few of them, but only a few and only slightly. As film critic Judith Crist, who is not in that category, says, "Once you have adapted yourself to your profession and adopted a life-style that will work with it, there is no reason for you ever to give it up." Many of the women are still active—working full-time, writing memoirs, or publishing freelance articles. One, in her seventies, still pulls all-nighters occasionally to meet deadlines. Their energy and stamina impressed me repeatedly

Introduction

and probably should be considered a requirement for a reporter.

The women had many suggestions for would-be journalists. One strong recommendation was to learn at least one foreign language. It's easier to acquire a foreign language when you're young, and the more languages you know, the easier it is to learn others. Whether you master the technical requirements of journalism in journalism school or on the job, a broad, solid liberal arts education is essential. A reporter can't know too much about literature, history, economics, geography, music, politics, science, poetry. Writing practice, ideally at least a thousand words a day, and wide reading are also important for students of journalism.

Because the number of newspapers is dwindling, and more of them are being taken over by large chains, it would be a good idea to develop several skills or specialties. Future reporters will have more opportunities in television than these women had, for example, and might be wise to prepare for work in broadcast as well as print journalism. Even many of the women in this book worked in several different journalistic fields. After her newspaper days, Marie Torre hosted a popular television talk show, "Contact," which was among her most gratifying work. She found that helping people, as with alerting them to a new medical treatment, was deeply satisfying and that this happened often in television.

Even though newsroom typewriters are giving way to computer terminals and wireless machines have been replaced by satellites, the achievements of these pioneers are

INTRODUCTION

a valuable legacy to young journalists. Women still have pioneering work to do—with all the challenge, hard work, and excitement it involves—but they can learn from those who went before.

Part One

CHAPTER 1

Emma Bugbee —
VOTES FOR WOMEN

Emma Bugbee is one of the few reporters still living who covered the campaign for votes for women in the early twentieth century. This campaign, also known as the women's suffrage movement, improved the status of women reporters who covered it. The New York Tribune, where Emma Bugbee worked for fifty-five years, allowed women reporters to move their desks into the city room (the main newsroom) in 1915. They had been in a separate upstairs office until then. Although women handled the daily coverage of the suffrage movement, men usually reported on marches and protests when they were front-page news.

Women marched in parades and picketed the White House, a new tactic at that time, and finally won the right to vote when the Nineteenth Amendment to the Constitution was ratified in 1920. Bugbee describes another advance, the start of the five-day work week, which came in the next decade as a result of Franklin D. Roosevelt's reforms. The six-day work week had been the norm until then.

In a way, Emma Bugbee started work a day late. When she began her job as the *Tribune correspondent from Barnard Col-*

PART ONE

lege, her editor said she wished Bugbee had been there to cover a story the day before. It was only fitting, then, that on her last day at the Tribune, *she was asked to work the day after her "retirement." The assignment was to cover the dedication of a bench in honor of Eleanor Roosevelt, whom Bugbee had covered regularly when she was First Lady. Emma Bugbee was so fond of her work, and of Eleanor Roosevelt, that she accepted the assignment eagerly.*

It all began long ago when I was at Barnard College. They had a press club, and I thought it would be fun to belong to that. The press club sent news of Barnard events to the newspapers. I selected the *Tribune*, you see. (It wasn't called the *Herald Tribune* then.)

I wrote the *Tribune* a letter. It said, "I'd like to be your correspondent at Barnard College." And the day after that I got a letter from the women's page editor saying, "Where were you yesterday? We wanted you to cover the basketball game." That was my first assignment.

When I was graduated from college, I went back to my hometown, Methuen, Massachusetts. I soon got a letter from New York saying that my friend, Eva vom Baur, who had gotten a permanent job on the *Tribune*, was going to Germany for a month to visit her grandparents. I was asked if I'd like to substitute for her for that month of August while she was away. Of course I was just delighted to move back to New York.

There I was, doing regular work for the *Tribune*, when Eva wrote that she had decided to stay in Germany for the winter. She was giving up her job, so they took me on as a substitute. She and I joke about it to this day. She said, "I lent you my job for a month, and you kept it for fifty years!" She never stopped teasing me. But she came back eventually and got to be editor of the women's page of the *New York Sun*. Everybody thinks I was high in journalism, but there were eleven newspapers in New York, and they all had at least one woman on the staff. And we *all* covered the votes-for-women campaign. That was our main job.

We went around every afternoon to the various headquarters of groups such as the National Woman Suffrage Assocation, the New York State Women's Association, and the New York City Votes for Women Association. There was no such thing as a press agent in those days. The head of the organization handed out the news. For example, if she'd had a letter from somebody important saying that that person liked or did not like the idea of votes for women, she'd come out and tell us the news.

The women's suffrage movement was just *boiling* in those years. We had two Fifth Avenue parades in New York. They were parades of women dressed all in white. The women carried banners saying, "Votes for Women." They were appealing to the New York state legislature, particularly, to adopt this suffrage measure. Then their representatives in Congress would have to vote the same way when the amendment came before the whole Congress.

After women got the vote, they had to keep on working for certain other rights. The Equal Rights Amendment is a natural outgrowth of the votes-for-women campaign. The National Woman's Party was founded by Alice Paul in 1913. The party drafted the Equal Rights Amendment and managed to have it introduced in Congress for forty-

PART ONE

nine consecutive years until it cleared both the house and Senate in 1972.

Oh, I'm for it of course. It's so simple. There's nothing to it, really. It just says that equal rights under the law shall not be denied or abridged on account of sex. That's all there is to it. And *some* of the people are so scared. They say the Equal Rights Amendment is going to turn the world upside down, the same way people were scared about votes for women.

People used to say, "Ohhhhhhh. Women shouldn't be going to the polls. Supposin' they had a sick baby at home?"

And we said, "That means they should never go to church either. They might have a sick baby!" Mrs. Carrie Chapman Catt, one of the famous suffragists, used to say that the antisuffragists talked as if women had sick babies every day of their lives, from twenty-one years on until they died, they had a sick baby at home!

I didn't notice any discrimination against me, if there was any. There were some limitations I just took for granted, such as the fact that I was covering the famous women of the period and not particularly the famous men. I did ask the women if they believed in votes for women. But I just took it for granted that I covered the women; I did cover almost all the famous women.

Once in a while it would be more than just a suffrage meeting or a suffrage parade. I went up in an airplane with Amelia Earhart, the well-known early aviator, one night when she took Mrs. Roosevelt up to see the lights of Washington. And I covered a murder trial. It was such a silly one. I think that's probably why they sent me!

I think it's interesting to note how hard we worked and

Emma Bugbee

how we took it for granted that we worked that hard. It's just the way it was. And we *loved* it, you see. We worked six days a week, right up through Saturday night if necessary. If anything was happening, if women's suffragists were having a meeting somewhere, why, we had to go, even on Saturday night. And we had late press. We could get a story into the paper up to midnight or one o'clock, even. Yet we thought it was *w o n d e r f u l!*

Then when the five-day week came in—it was one of Roosevelt's reforms—the old guard at the newspapers thought it was terrible, because then we had two days off a week instead of just one. My city editor said, "Why I *love* newspaper work."

I said, "Well, I do too. But I can love it five days a week just as well as six."

When I retired, a story about me appeared in the last paper, as such, that the *Tribune* published. There had been a farewell lunch and I had said good-bye to everybody. Then notice came into the city desk that a memorial bench for Mrs. Roosevelt on the grounds of the United Nations was going to be dedicated the next afternoon. That would have been Saturday afternoon, and I'd retired on Friday. There was a wonderful girl on the city desk who was assistant city editor at that time. She said, "Why don't we have Emma cover Mrs. Roosevelt's dedication of the bench? We'll do it on a freelance basis."

Sure enough, that's what I did. There was this great big marble bench with the name ELEANOR ROOSEVELT carved in it. I was sitting on the bench taking notes, and our photographer got that picture. They ran the story that I had writ-

PART ONE

ten and also the story about my years on the paper in the last issue that the *Tribune* ever published.

CHAPTER 2

Kathleen McLaughlin —
Covering Chicago Gangsters

Kathleen McLaughlin and I met at the Newswomen's Club of New York, the night of one of its annual Christmas parties, to talk about her work covering Chicago gangsters. It was a festive occasion, with many newswomen of all ages, homemade refreshments, and holiday decorations. (McLaughlin's friendships with her former colleagues made it possible for me to locate and interview many of them for this book.)

We sat in a downstairs lobby to talk about the shootings, assassinations, and other gangland activities she covered for the Chicago Tribune *in the 1920s. She refers to this era, when organized crime was in its heyday, as "the purple chapters of gangsterism." One of the most unforgettable characters she wrote about, Big Tim Murphy, is described in this chapter.*

Chicago was at its most exciting as a newspaper town then, with several competing papers, and Kathleen McLaughlin found her experience at the Tribune *to be an ideal journalism education. She had decided as a child that she wanted to be a reporter and*

27

PART ONE

eventually became one of the first women to work for the New York Times. *At the* Times, *she reported important stories in the United States and abroad. In another chapter, she tells about covering Eleanor Roosevelt. McLaughlin also went abroad as a war correspondent near the end of the second world war. Her ship had to zigzag across the Atlantic to avoid being hit by enemy submarines, but she reached Europe safely and covered the opening of the international Nuremberg trials for war crimes.*

She reported on Germany and witnessed the revival of the German economy after the war. She became fascinated with the relationship between economics and politics and spent several years recently covering economic news at the United Nations.

When we finished talking it was late at night, but McLaughlin learned that her friends were still gathered upstairs and returned to join the party.

Reporting always interested me from the time I was extremely small and just learning to read. I can remember sprawling on my stomach on the living room floor, spelling out the *Atchison* (Kansas) *Daily Globe* items and asking my mother, "Who finds out what happened?"

She said, "They're called reporters."

I said, "When I grow up, I want to be a reporter." And I never changed my mind. I found it magnetic to find out what was happening and to tell it, preferably in grammatical form. I'm sure that I'm a throwback to what my mother would have been and done, except that she was born a little bit too soon.

I actually began reporting on the *Atchison Daily Globe* in Atchison, Kansas, which in those days long ago was a very valuable property and a prize-winning country town jour-

Kathleen McLaughlin

nal. Not too long after I started working for the *Globe*, I went to Chicago on a vacation with the idea that I would apply to various papers, anticipating that when I came back in about five years with enough experience, I would know how to go about applying for a job in Chicago. So I took a few of the by-lined stories I had written for the *Daily Globe*.

I went to the *Chicago Tribune* on an experimental basis, as it were, asked for an interview, and to my surprise, I got one. To my consternation, I was told that I could come to work the next day. I was totally unprepared for such a development and protested that after all, I had to go back to my hometown, Atchison, to collect my clothes and to make a, shall I say, mannerly exit. I was stopped cold by the day city editor who said, "Do you want to work here or don't you?"

I said, "Of course I do."

He said, "All right. Resign by telegram." (We didn't have good telephone communication in those days.) "And if you want to work here, show up tomorrow."

Well, it was quite a confrontation. But I summoned my courage and resigned by telegram. I went to work on the *Chicago Tribune* as a general reporter in 1925, the days of the purple chapters of gangsterism in Chicago. While I must confess that I lost fifteen pounds in my first two months on the *Tribune*, just out of worry and anxiety and trying to keep up, at the end of that time I was getting excellent assignments. At the end of six months I had a by-line, which meant that my job was secure.

One of the best schools of journalism I could have had was the *Chicago Tribune* staff. Did they knock you into

PART ONE

shape, tell you where you got off! I encountered incomparable people who had backgrounds I just didn't have, but which sort of shed on me.

I began to get assignments to cover the trials of the well-known gangsters and the many shootings and assassinations in the gangster world. I must confess that I've spent a great deal of my life, a decade in Chicago on the *Chicago Tribune*, sitting in law courts covering trial after trial. It's extremely instructive if you don't know anything about law. If you sit long enough in a courtroom and hear the prosecutor and the defense attorneys contending, you absorb the basic principles of law.

So in that particularly purple decade, most of the reporters on the *Tribune* got one opportunity after another to cover these gangsters, to report their idiosyncrasies, their convictions, the color, the danger, the risks of their lives. To borrow a phrase from another woman reporter, "They lived dangerously and died violently." It was characteristic of that era in Chicago.

Fortunately, the *Chicago Tribune* in those days gave its women reporters precisely the same chance the men had, and it was wonderfully appreciated. If you were good enough you got a top assignment. It didn't matter whether you were Miss or Mrs. or Mr. on the city editor's assignment sheet.

Things being as they were in Chicago in those days, there were plenty of places to go and plenty of speed applied to get there. That was a little bit after the era when the circulation war between the Chicago newspapers had developed. The competition was but *terrific*. We encountered all sorts of trickery, and there were other names I could put to it! The tactics were uninhibited—impersonation of police officers by the reporters, that sort of thing. If you happened to be a naive cub reporter, a beginner, it was just too bad because you got educated in a *hurry*.

Among my really pleasant memories of Chicago, believe it or not, was a man called Big Tim Murphy, who was a long, tall Irishman, six feet four, a terrific wit, a labor leader, with a very, shall I say, checkered reputation. I could never be convinced, ever, that he took the life of any human being. He was just too, too human. Big Tim would have been a character in whatever era he lived. As he used to say, "I graduated from swimming school." He had little formal education, but his native intelligence was a *delight*.

Big Tim was, I must say, a part of *my* education. Here was a man who was apparently one of the most loving and tender husbands I have ever known about. He and his wife, Florence, who was a big, Junoesque, beautiful blonde, had eight children born, not one of whom survived more than twenty-four hours. All of Big Tim's love of children was poured into two youngsters he and his wife adopted.

Yet he was arrested, convicted, and jailed for at least three years for the robbery of a mail train in Chicago, in which a large number of government bonds disappeared. I was assigned to go to Leavenworth, Kansas, to write a story about his release from prison. He gave me an interview and made a remark I'll never forget. He indirectly acknowledged his guilt in the affair for which he'd been convicted, saying, characteristically, "I'm never going to monkey any more with Uncle Sam, with his striped pants and his billy-goat beard."

He was one of those characters you meet once in a

PART ONE

lifetime. There was so much good in him, along with his, shall I say, questionable operations. He was obviously on the wrong side of the law any number of times. I recall one occasion when I was assigned to interview him at the office he had in the Loop in Chicago. I was a little bit late, so I saw him come out. You couldn't miss him, after all, with that height. So I was hurrying back of him trying to catch up. I saw the behavior of a Chicago gangster: looking back over this shoulder and then over that shoulder, alert for enemies.

Not too long after that episode, gangsters rang the doorbell at his home, or called him to the door. (There was almost continuous warfare in those days between gangsters involved in various labor unions.) From the car at the curb, they sprayed Big Tim with machine-gun bullets, and he fell on the lawn. That was it for Big Tim.

After my ten years in Chicago, I moved to New York. This was about a month after the death of the publisher of the *New York Times,* Adolph Ochs. I didn't realize it, but I had arrived at rather an opportune time. According to, I guess, both record and legend, Mr. Ochs was not very happy about women in the newspaper field. Fortunately for me, Arthur Hays Sulzberger, who succeeded his father-in-law as publisher, had a completely different point of view.

I went on the *New York Times* general news staff in 1935. At the moment, I was the only woman reporter in the newsroom. Not that I hadn't had predecessors, because I had. There were some quite famous gals a long time back —some of them outstanding reporters. But at the time that

Kathleen McLaughlin

I arrived, I was the only woman in the newsroom. And if I may say so, and I will say so, you could have cut the ice with a hatchet. I can remember only one reporter on the staff, whose name was Marshall Newton, who was nice enough to come over to me and say, "We're delighted you're here, and welcome." For the rest of them, I just wasn't there, for months on months.

But primarily, I've been grateful for the camaraderie of many wonderful journalists. You know, when you're on a big story, a really big story, with enough variety and number of newspapers to reflect the differences of the people covering it, it's a journalism school in itself. That happened to me time after time. I wrote my story, and the other people wrote their stories. You saw what you'd missed and how you'd muffed this angle and that angle, what they had that you didn't have. This is the kind of journalism school that is just beyond price. It was wonderful fun and incredibly interesting, and an education, I would say, beyond any degree I could ever get elsewhere.

CHAPTER 3

Eleanor Roosevelt and Her Press Group

Eleanor Roosevelt wrote a column, "My Day," which was carried in newspapers throughout the country. Her husband criticized it for being more like a diary than a column, but it was popular with readers and she filed her copy religiously, no matter where she was. She dictated a column during one son's wedding reception in Delaware. As her "press group," the women who wrote about her regularly, would say, "That was Mrs. R."

Eleanor Roosevelt belongs in this book because of what she did for other women journalists, rather than for her own column. She started holding press conferences for women only, which forced major newspapers and wire services to assign women, and in some cases hire women, to cover them. At the first such conference, Mrs. Roosevelt passed around a box of candied fruits to try to hide her nervousness. She knew she was going to make news, though, and the conferences became an institution.

Among the women who covered her were Kathleen McLaughlin of the Chicago Tribune *and later the* New York Times, *Emma*

Eleanor Roosevelt

Bugbee of the New York Herald Tribune, *and Dorothy Ducas of International News Service. As they recall some of their experiences reporting on Eleanor Roosevelt, their affection and admiration for her come through clearly.*

Eleanor Roosevelt and many of the women who covered her became good friends during Franklin D. Roosevelt's unprecedented twelve years as President. But not all of them admired her completely. One reporter remembered being annoyed by her "infernal knitting" as she talked with women journalists. Another said that "for a plain woman with a dreadful voice, she had a considerable amount of charm."

This First Lady served as her husband's eyes, ears, and legs because he was often confined to a wheelchair as a result of polio. When she visited a coal mine to learn about the working conditions of the miners, many members of her press group went along. Four reporters, including Emma Bugbee and Dorothy Ducas, went with her to Puerto Rico on another mission for the President.

Eleanor Roosevelt was concerned about all people, and contributed to racial equality as well as to opportunities for women reporters. Kathleen McLaughlin describes Mrs. Roosevelt's defense of Marian Anderson, who was not allowed to sing at Constitution Hall in Washington, D. C., because she is black. Eleanor Roosevelt took action by obtaining a permit to use the Lincoln Memorial, where Marian Anderson sang outdoors on Easter Sunday, 1939, in a triumphant recital before more than seventy-five thousand people.

PART ONE
Kathleen McLaughlin

The first Roosevelt election was in 1932. I had been covering political conventions for the *Chicago Tribune*, taking care of the women's news, naturally, for some time. My first view of Franklin Roosevelt was from the press box in the Chicago stadium in 1932, when he broke precedent after his nomination by flying to Chicago to accept. There was no television at that time. It was quite dramatic to sit in the press box in the stadium, which was filled, following the progress by radio of his motorcade from Midway Airport to the Chicago stadium. We'd listen, and they were at this point, then at this point, and at this point. Presently, they were outside the stadium, and presently, the nominee made his appearance on the arm of one of his sons.

Of course everyone knew that he'd been crippled by polio. But it was an experience to see this tremendously impressive man approach the rostrum, which was elevated above the press box, facing the assembly. He was swinging both legs, carefully but painfully, as he entered the rostrum, this hale and hearty and charismatic man. It was in this speech that he said, "I pledge you, I pledge myself a new deal for the American people." But at the moment I was assigned to women's news!

So I was waiting for the appearance of Eleanor Roosevelt. I must say I got a bit of a shock, because her husband and son had riveted all eyes as they approached the lectern. Mrs. Roosevelt was shrinking to the back rail of the elevated rostrum and leaning against it. I looked at her and I have to confess that my first thought was, "My God!"

She was so long and so tall. She was wearing black

cotton stockings and a very simple, unchic, straight-line dress—black, with red floral sprigs; a very large hat, rather flat-crowned; black gloves; and a pedestrian handbag. She was just sort of shrinking there in the shadow of her famous husband. All I could think of was, "What is the public going to think about her?"

The next morning at the Congress Hotel in Chicago, Mrs. Roosevelt gave a press conference. She was so utterly far from the type of retiring, quiet, mouselike presidential wives, that from then on, to me, she was one of the most vigorous, wonderful individuals I have ever encountered or ever will.

Emma Bugbee and I and a few other newswomen—Dorothy Ducas, Bess Furman, Ruby Black—well, I wouldn't attempt to name them all—but there was a little group of us who became very close to her and very warmly related. She was . . . well, she was . . . she was . . . just take my stammering for what I think of her. We saw her in every sort of condition, situation, crisis, and she came through in every one of them. She was a marvelous, marvelous person. She definitely had very special qualities. One aspect of her development, which has been on the record for years, is her terrific training in the League of Women Voters. The members of this nonpolitical group never took a position on a public problem until they had studied it for two years, so that they felt they knew what they were doing if they took a position.

Mrs. Roosevelt was very involved in this whole training program and in the philosophy behind it: that you don't plunge into something until you know what it's about and what could happen one way or the other. It taught her a

PART ONE

great deal, and it directed so many of her actions and her philosophies and her decisions when she was the President's wife. That meticulous attitude: you first find out what's involved, then you make your decision, and then you take a position. I would pay homage to the League of Women Voters for their contribution to her political education, as she so often did.

From 1932 on, I covered her for the *Chicago Tribune* from Washington and later from New York for the *New York Times*. I was a member of the Women's National Press Club in Washington, as was Emma Bugbee. We used to go down to the club's annual stunt parties. Because Emmy and I were from out of town, Mrs. Roosevelt would invite us to stay at the White House, which is also an education.

One year, Emmy and I went to Washington for the Press Club stunt party, and we stayed in what was called the Yellow Room, on the second floor of the White House. We had tried to get the window open, and you know the White House is a very old house. This was long before it was rehabilitated during the Truman administration. We must have spent half an hour to forty-five minutes standing on this bench below these great French windows, tugging and tugging and tugging, just trying to get the window open. We couldn't. Finally we were so exhausted we just said, "Let's leave the door to the hall open." At the time, the President was on a cruise in the Caribbean.

So we went to bed with the door open. It was pretty late. I woke the next morning hearing "dulcet" tones from down the hall: "I want breakfast!" It was FDR.

I looked over and saw that Emmy was awake. I said, "Emmy, my God! The President's back, and we're not out of bed!" So we rushed and raced to get to the breakfast table. Of course they didn't wait for anybody. FDR was sitting at one end of the table. James Roosevelt and his wife, Betsy, were still married, and Betsy was there beside the President with this little table where FDR loved to make his own coffee. Mrs. R. was sitting opposite, at the other end of the table. When we got there, very apologetic, there were probably ten or twelve people at the breakfast table.

It was just before the famous incident when the Daughters of the American Revolution refused to let Marian Anderson sing in their Constitution Hall in Washington. You see, FDR hadn't been briefed at all. So Mrs. Roosevelt was trying to help him catch up with what had happened. She was telling him about the DAR refusing to let Marian Anderson sing in their hall because she's a Negro. And he said, chin cocked high, in one of the most characteristic moments I have ever witnessed, "I suppose you would call her a coloratura soprano?"

She said, "Oh, Franklin!" Then everyone laughed, but she took action. Marian Anderson sang before a huge crowd of people outdoors on the steps of the Lincoln Memorial.

Emma Bugbee

The *New York Herald Tribune* sent me down to cover Eleanor Roosevelt's part in FDR's first inauguration in March, 1933. She held a press conference the Monday after the inauguration and said, "Well, next week, I'm going to

PART ONE

have you all upstairs. We'll have a little more room and a little more privacy."

She showed us around all over upstairs—the President's room and her room adjoining it, and the rooms for the most important visiting celebrities. We asked, "Can we write this?" And she said, "Why, of course. This house belongs to the people, and they have a right to know what it looks like."

So we did. We wrote it all. My office was so impressed that we got all this news and that she was going to treat the press this way. They said, "Get yourself a hotel in Washington and prepare to cover Mrs. Roosevelt whenever she is in Washington. Just prepare to cover her wherever she is." Once Eleanor Roosevelt got to the White House, every move she made was astonishing to the American people. There'd never been a First Lady like that, you see.

She established a press conference for women only for two reasons. One, there was a depression, and if she had a press conference for women only, it would save some women's jobs, some women who might otherwise be dismissed, or it might help women get jobs. And two, the White House news had formerly kind of *leaked* out. You know, somebody knew the cook, and the cook told some secret. Mrs. Roosevelt didn't like that. She wanted everybody to get all the news there was and get it at the same time. And she knew she was going to make news. (Mrs. Roosevelt's activities were heavily ridiculed by the anti-Roosevelt newspapers, and more than one woman had to change her job because she would not write articles ridiculing Eleanor Roosevelt.)

We went down into Appalachia with her once to visit

the coal mines. We were met at the train. The people of the town turned out; everywhere she went the people lined up. They had washed the streets the night before and put out flowers everywhere. There was some trouble about working conditions in the coal mines, and she wanted to see exactly how they were. The day we went into the coal mines, everybody was told to wear blue jeans because it would be dirty. But she wouldn't wear blue jeans because she knew the photographers would catch her. There was no sense in our wearing blue jeans either, because we were in a trolley car. It was decorated with bright new bunting. I don't think we even got out of it. If we did, it was just to step around a little. We didn't dig any coal!

Several women reporters also went with her on a trip to Puerto Rico in 1934. She had to consent to our going, but she liked us! The President sent her down there to find out about the condition of the women garment workers. Puerto Rican underwear for women—nightgowns and chemises—was much cheaper than American-made underwear, you see. The reason was that the Puerto Rican women worked in huts up in the woods where the light was very poor. Many of them went blind because of it.

About ten years later, I saw President and Mrs. Roosevelt together for the last time. I'll never forget it. It was on election night in 1944, when FDR had run in spite of poor health and political opposition. We were all at the President's home in Hyde Park, New York. Every election night, the Hyde Park neighbors always came out with torchlights and serenaded the family. I can still see that tableau. It was kind of a misty, cold night, and the Roosevelts stood out there on the veranda of the Hyde Park

PART ONE

house. He always wore a long, blue navy cape. He loved that cape. I can still see her pulling that cape up around his shoulders and neck to keep him warm. That's a memory that I treasure very much.

Dorothy Ducas

Emma Bugbee and I were covering Mrs. Roosevelt at the same time. We were members of her press conference. I began covering her in about 1928 when her husband was governor of New York. I covered her whenever she came to New York City. Then when FDR ran for President, I covered her for International News Service right through the presidential campaign. For the inauguration and the first year, I flew to Washington and was a member of her first press conference group. It was 1933 when they moved into the White House, and of course he was elected four times. I continued covering her activities for eight years, then worked with her when I went to Washington, D.C., to work for the Office of War Information.

When she became First Lady, Mrs. Roosevelt had a group of women covering her activities. She wouldn't let the men come in. She didn't think it was fair that presidential news conferences were for men only, so she had her conferences just for women. I was one of the original ones. She had a weekly conference, and we went every week.

She never treated reporters as most political figures do. After she got to know us, we became her friends. As a matter of fact, toward the end of that first administration, some of the editors complained that the women in her press

Eleanor Roosevelt

group couldn't do an unbiased story about Mrs. Roosevelt because we so admired her. If she did anything wrong, they felt we wouldn't be able to see it. I think that was unfair, but there were people who felt that way.

I never really disagreed with her, I must admit. Well, yes I did once when she was urging funds for some kind of make-work program for a dancer during the second world war. I thought this was most inappropriate for the times. I thought there were better programs we could put people to work in than a modern dance group. But I never argued with her about it.

She was a women who cared *only* about human values. She was a good politician, but she wasn't nearly as shrewd as people gave her credit for being. A lot of people took advantage of her. I know several who used her kindness to get themselves ahead in the world. She was a very warm-hearted woman. . . . We used to tease her. She had sort of an awkward gait, and you could always see her corset in back. . . .

Only four reporters went with Mrs. Roosevelt to Puerto Rico in 1934. We landed in Saint Thomas in the Virgin Islands. It was very hot, and too late to do anything about swimming. But we all said, "Let's go swimming first thing tomorrow morning before we start doing anything else."

Mrs. Roosevelt said, "Oh, I'd love to. We'll all go together, before we do anything else."

She was staying at the governor's palace overlooking the harbor, and we were in a very old hotel nearby. At six-thirty the next morning, she knocked on our door. Bess Furman's and my room had swinging doors, so when Mrs.

Emma Bugbee at the beginning of her career. Now in her nineties, she still reports for *Barnard Alumnae* magazine on the activities of her class of 1909.

Kathleen McLaughlin, left, women's news editor, and Helene Lazareff, assistant editor, at the *New York Times* office, 1943.

Kathleen McLaughlin, right, with Gen. Walter Bedel Smith, reporting for the *New York Times* at a displaced person's camp in Germany in late 1945.

Emma Bugbee dressed as Abigail Adams at one of many parties Eleanor Roosevelt gave for newspaperwomen. Emma Bugbee sent this photograph to Mrs. Roosevelt as a Christmas card.

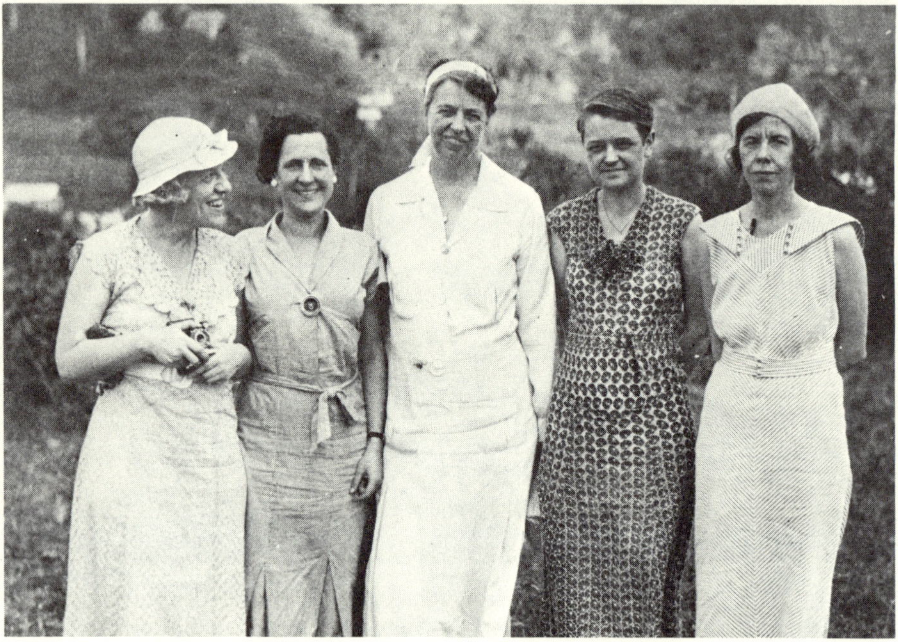

Courtesy: Franklin D. Roosevelt Library

Eleanor Roosevelt and members of her press group in Puerto Rico, March, 1934. Left to right Emma Bugbee, Dorothy Ducas, Eleanor Roosevelt, Ruby Black, Bess Furman.

Eleanor Roosevelt, left, and Dorothy Ducas.

Courtesy: Franklin D. Roosevelt Library

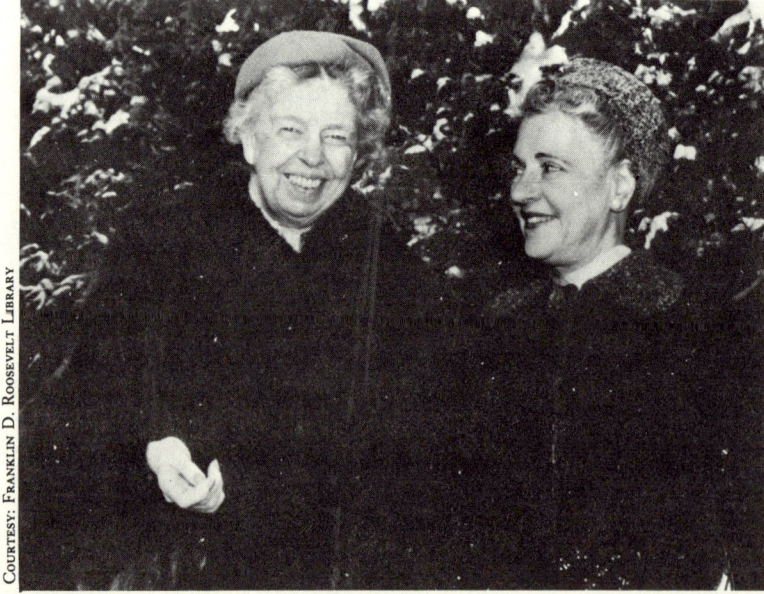

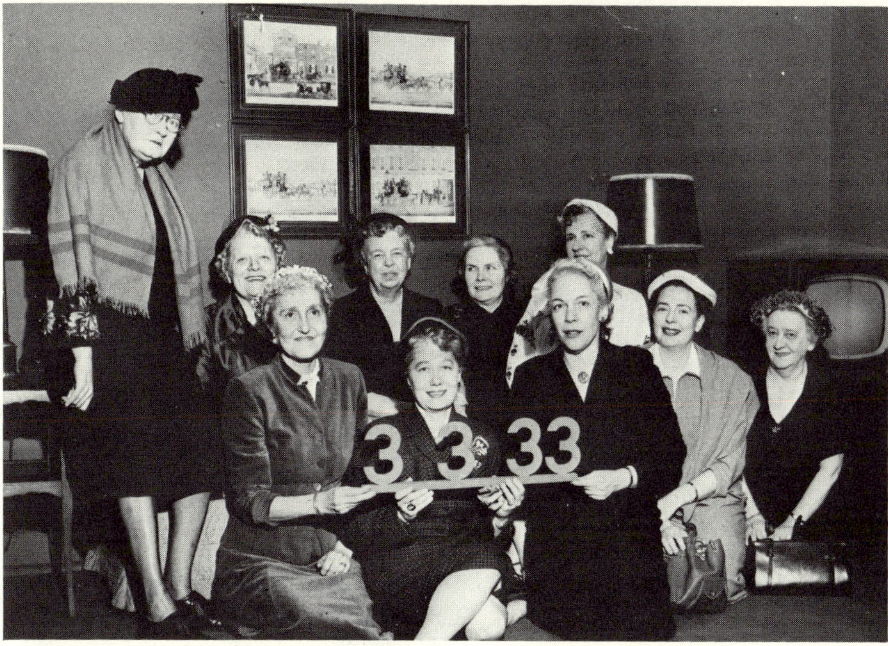

PHOTO COSMO-SILEO, COURTESY: FRANKLIN D. ROOSEVELT LIBRARY

Eleanor Roosevelt in 1953 at the twentieth anniversary luncheon of her first press conference in Washington, D.C. The numbers *3 3 33* stands for March 3, 1933. In the back row, left to right, are Lorena Hickok, Emma Bugbee, Eleanor Roosevelt, Kathleen McLaughlin, and Dorothy Ducas.

Twentieth anniversary luncheon of Eleanor Roosevelt's first press conference. The luncheon was held in 1953 at the Algonquin Hotel in New York City.

PHOTO COSMO-SILEO, COURTESY: FRANKLIN D. ROOSEVELT LIBRARY

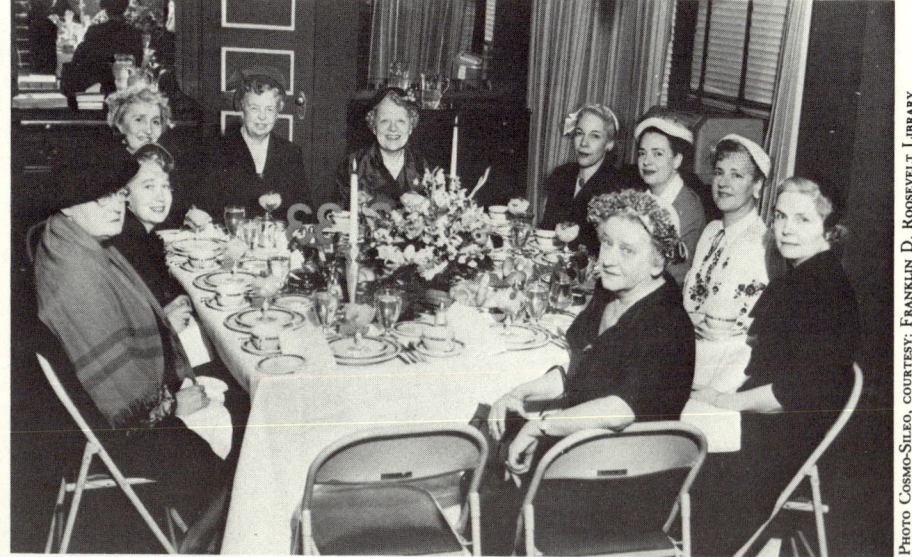

Mildred Gilman in her rented diving suit, shortly before she went down to the bottom of the Hackensack River on February 3, 1930. An excerpt from the story she wrote about the experience reads: "From the minute your eighteen pound lead shoes leave the last rung of the ladder and your heavy canvas rubber mittens let loose their friendly clasp, you're in a remote, terribly different world. Going down-down-down, gliding— wondering what would happen to you if the pumps stop working, or you get air in your joints, called the 'bends,' or that awful thing happens that squeezes all of you into the helmet. Down—down—down."

Norma Abrams Miley in the living room of her New York City apartment in 1976.

Eleanor Roosevelt

R. woke us, we could see her feet in the hall. She said, "Lazy bones, get up! Time to go swimming." We all went with her. She had a big limousine at her disposal. We went down to a secluded beach. There wasn't a soul in sight. There was only one big dressing room for men and another big dressing room for women. Naturally we stood back and said, "You go first, Mrs. Roosevelt."

She said, "Nonsense. We'll all go together." So we went in and put on our bathing suits without false modesty in this big room. She was one of the girls.

A Puerto Rican caricaturist on a Spanish-language newspaper in San Juan did a caricature of Mrs. R. It was a good caricature, but it exaggerated her protruding "Roosevelt" teeth. The governor of Puerto Rico was upset and called the paper, saying that was an insulting way to greet the First Lady. The publisher apologized. Later we learned that the caricaturist was fired because of this. Bess and I were horrified about the man losing his job, so we told Mrs. Roosevelt. She called the publisher and demanded that he be put back on. She didn't mind the cartoon because it was accurate. She saved his job.

The following year, 1935, my younger son was born. There was an announcement of it in the paper. Next day, a big vase of flowers arrived at New York Hospital from the White House. The nurses made a big fuss over them. Then, just two or three days before I was to go (you stayed in the hospital for two weeks then), one of the nurses came dashing down the corridor: "Mrs. Herzog"—my name is also Mrs. Herzog—"guess who's here? Mrs. Roosevelt!"

Because she was the First Lady, the whole hospital was in an uproar. They brought her in—she was perfectly natu-

PART ONE

ral—and left us alone. But you could see them hanging around the door to my room trying to listen. She said, "I wonder if I could see the baby." They were delighted to take her down to the glass-enclosed nursery at the end of the corridor.

She came back and said, "Oh, Dorothy. He's lovely." He was. Tom was a very pretty baby. He had red hair even when he was born—little pink tufts all over his head. Mrs. R. said, "What do you think those foolish nurses asked me? They asked me if I would like to go inside the nursery, as if my germs weren't the same as everybody else's!" Of course she refused to go in.

I had my marriage and my children and worked all during that time without any sense of guilt whatsoever. This new crop of girls seems to always feel guilty about wanting to have careers. I don't know why. I never did. My husband backed me a hundred percent. That's a big part of it. He knew I was *happy* in what I was doing.

I tried staying home for a couple of months when the boys were young. I was miserable, and I was a miserable mother. Once back at work, I was a better mother, more relaxed. I always made enough money to hire the right person to take care of the boys—someone intelligent, educated, athletic, and fun. It worked!

I was invited many times to the White House as Mrs. Roosevelt's personal guest. When you were invited as a guest, you didn't write about what you heard. I remember one time my elder son and I were invited to Hyde Park for lunch with the President. He got word at the luncheon table of the fire and sinking of a ship called S.S. *Vestris*. He was so angry. He said, "When will they stop building wooden ships? We don't have to have wood on the ships so they burn up." Oh, he was furious. That would have made a very good comment on the story, but I never used it because I was there as a guest. I would have thought that was taking advantage.

In 1962, those of us who were left of Mrs. Roosevelt's press group suddenly were invited to lunch at her New York City home in the East Sixties. Nothing was indicated as to the occasion. Bess Furman came up from Washington, where she lived, and stayed with me overnight. I asked Bess and I asked Emma Bugbee, "Is this an anniversary or something?" And it wasn't. We couldn't figure out why we were invited. All of us who could, went. Kathleen McLaughlin was there too.

After lunch, Bess and I were walking over to my apartment and I said, "I don't understand why she did this."

Bess said, "Oh, I think she just got lonesome for us, wanted to see us."

That's the last time I saw Mrs. Roosevelt. Two months later she was dead. After Mrs. Roosevelt died, Maureen Carr, who was then her secretary, said, "That isn't why you girls were invited. She knew at the time that she was going to die. She was saying good-bye." I thought it rather poignant that she thought enough of her press conference girls to want to say good-bye to us.

CHAPTER 4

Mildred Gilman —
Stunt Reporter, Sob Sister, and Foreign Correspondent

Mildred Gilman was, among other things, a "sob sister," one of the women reporters who wrote emotional, colorful stories about murders, trials, and celebrities in the early 1900s. The best-known of her eight books is Sob Sister, *which was made into a movie that appears occasionally on television.*

Gilman, who today is Mrs. Robert Wohlforth, is also a novelist, reporter, and foreign correspondent. She was the first woman editor of the Wisconsin Literary Magazine *at the University of Wisconsin. She wrote her first novel,* Fig Leaves, *when she was just out of college, and wrote* Headlines *before she ever worked on a newspaper.*

Gilman packed adventure after adventure into her three years as a reporter on the New York Journal, *"America's Greatest Evening Newspaper," as its masthead said. She descended to the bottom of a New Jersey river in a heavy, old-fashioned diving suit, and made the first radiotelephone call from an airplane, when flying was still a daring thing to do. She was once picked up and grilled as a suspect in a murder case when a telephone operator overheard her tell her husband about a body stuffed into a suitcase.*

The day the stock market crashed to a new low on October 29,

Mildred Gilman

1929, known as "Black Tuesday," Gilman was on the balcony over the Stock Exchange. Her city editor had sent her down to Wall Street "to see what is going on." She was supposed to find a "woman's angle" in everything and the long "monster" headline on her story read:

WIVES, SHOW GIRLS, TEACHERS,
   STENOS—ALL HIT BY MARKET
WRITER TELLS OF BEDLAM ON STREET
Havoc Ruins Dreams of Wealth
and Affects Women All Over World

Gilman was also one of Eleanor Roosevelt's "girls," reporting for the Washington (D.C.) Herald.

Sensational stories were given great space in newspapers in the years between the two world wars. "We printed so little international news," she said, "because we never dreamed another war would be possible after what we thought was 'the war to end wars.' " But when she got a chance to go to Germany, Gilman took it. The Gestapo, the German secret police, ordered her out of Germany after she interviewed Nazi leader Hermann Göring, spent four days and nights in a women's work camp, and talked with a man recently released from the Dachau concentration camp.

Following her years as a reporter in New York, Washington, D.C., and Nazi Germany, she continued to write—novels, articles about the Planned Parenthood Association, short stories, magazine articles. She wrote one of the first New Yorker *profiles, which was on Paul Robeson, the black singer and actor.*

Gilman has had her fill of stunt reporting and won't fly at all

PART ONE

now, although she still writes and stays physically active by bicycling three miles a day. She won't tell her age for fear that people will start helping her across the street!

My mother taught me to write before I went to school and just let me know I was going to be a writer. She wanted to be one herself and was frustrated. I was a very docile child. I kind of liked the idea. I was keeping a diary by the time I was in first grade. I still have it. It was all sentences beginning with "I," in letters about two inches high!

I was very bored in school. My mother had this weird idea that if you used your brain too much you wore it out. She never let me advance with the bright kids, never allowed me to skip a grade. It was dreadful, particularly since I was tall for my age. I developed a third ear so I could tell when the teacher was going to call on me. The rest of the time I'd write books of poetry and autobiographies. I wrote constantly. Once in a while I'd get caught.

At the University of Wisconsin I took almost every English course, American literature, English literature, Shakespeare, and a creative writing course that required one to write a thousand words a day: a story, essay, or article. This gave me a beautiful grounding in writing. I would advise this for anyone interested in becoming a writer. After that daily thousand words, nothing phases you. It was a continuation of my mother's training.

My first job on a New York newspaper was landed by a fluke. I had a letter of introduction from a friend, Cedric Worth, city editor of the racing sheet, the *Morning Telegraph*, to his friend Victor Watson, city editor of William Randolph Hearst's *Morning American*. This letter praised

Mildred Gilman

me as a writer, mentioned my book, *Headlines*, and said I was a "rare find." In the Hearst Building, where the *Morning American* was located, I got off the elevator on the sixth instead of the fifth floor and mistakenly delivered the letter to Amster Spiro, city editor of the *New York Journal*. He had read and liked *Headlines* and assumed I had wide newspaper experience. Also, he felt he was putting one over on his competitor, Victor Watson.

Spiro said, "What will you work for?"

I said, "I have never worked for a newspaper for less than a hundred dollars a week," not adding that I had never worked for a newspaper at all. The going rate for men was sixty dollars.

"I'll try you," he said. "Begin tomorrow at nine."

Big dramatic stories were easy for a novelist to cover. My first story was very dramatic, the return of the survivors of the sunken S. S. *Vestris*, on the freighter *American Shipper*, to New York Harbor. More than a hundred passengers had drowned. The *Vestris* captain had delayed the SOS too long to try to avoid the high salvage charges that would be owed if he had to be towed ashore or aided in any other way. The survivors told dramatic horror stories. I was the only female on that first story, trying to act wise and experienced.

A rope ladder was lowered to our tiny cutter from the huge *American Shipper*. "You go up first," my colleagues said gallantly. If you have ever tried ascending a rope ladder clinging to the side of a huge ship, you will know it is hopeless. First I dropped my handbag, spilling everything. My very short skirt billowed out. The men below clapped and whistled. Finally I couldn't move; I was stuck to the

PART ONE

ship's side. From above and below the men howled. The ladder—with me still on it—was lowered to the cutter and the regular wooden ladder let down. That was the first but far from the last trick played on me. The male reporters teased me, but I couldn't have kept my job without their help. When they realized I had no experience, they helped me and covered for me whenever possible.

When real news was scarce, we created news. Sometimes the city editor thought up stories, like sending me to Columbia University to ask undergraduates what kind of women they would choose for wives, or accompanying a publicity-mad millionaire realtor, Daddy Browning, to the Bowery where he distributed five-dollar bills and warm caps to down-and-outers.

There was an "idea man," *Journal* reporter Henry Paynter, who thought up some grim and far-out stunts for me. One idea was to send me down to the bottom of the Hackensack River in New Jersey in an old-fashioned diving suit, the kind that weighed a couple of hundred pounds and had a heavy metal headpiece. We had great difficulty finding a diver who would lend his suit to a woman. There was a superstition that if a woman used it, death would follow. But business was poor for Morton Tredge. He needed the publicity. So he lent me his suit, full of blow-out patches.

The idea was that a diver named Peter Trans had gone down a few days earlier to investigate the cofferdam of a bridge being built in Canada. (A cofferdam is a watertight enclosure from which water is pumped to permit construction of a bridge.) His lines became fouled up, and he needed

Mildred Gilman

help. The only way he could be rescued was by someone else in a diving suit. No other diver was nearby, so he slowly suffocated. Henry Paynter wanted me to go down thirty feet to the bottom of the Hackensack River and inspect the cofferdam of a bridge, then under construction, and figure out how poor Peter Trans felt during those last terrible minutes.

They sent me down in the only diving suit within miles, so nothing could have saved me if I had needed help—perfect for registering Peter's last thoughts! Just before Morton put the heavy headpiece on me, he said, "Be sure to push that little valve near your right ear often, otherwise you will suffocate in your own carbon dioxide. Don't get excited and thrash around or you will cut yourself on the copper helmet and breastplate." That was all I needed to hear at the last minute. I registered Peter's panic perfectly. The only wonders of the deep that I saw were some tin cans and a discarded rubber boot. I pulled the wrong line as a signal to be brought to the surface, but they caught on and pulled me up anyway.

Henry thought up another nearly lethal story for me—a Prohibition feature. Prohibition of liquor during the twenties and thirties created crime just as traffic in narcotics creates crime these days. Innocent people were killed by sleuthing dry agents whose job was to enforce Prohibition. Bootleg wars to the death took place between rival gangs. Fifty-third Street in New York City between Fifth and Sixth avenues had so many basement speakeasies where liquor was sold illegally that the few private residences had signs on their doors: PRIVATE—THIS IS NOT A SPEAKEASY.

Henry figured out a way to trap the bootleggers who

PART ONE

were selling dangerous mixtures, those that included too much wood alcohol. He had Spiro send me with a male reporter to several suspect speakeasies where we ordered drinks and then secretly poured small amounts into marked bottles we carried with us. Of course we tasted the drinks, and sometimes took a chance and drank all of them. Once I had sharp pains behind my eyes because of the effects of the wood alcohol, but we both survived. Our boss, in a crusading spirit, had the bottled drinks tested and exposed the speakeasies whose weird mixtures were dangerous.

Many have asked why I took these assignments. First of all, I liked excitement and doing new things. Second, I was afraid I might be fired if I turned down an assignment. I knew I had to be better and more daring than anyone else to be the top gal reporter and earn my phenomenal pay.

There was another reason for my ambition. I was the second girl in my family, born a year after the first one died. Four years later came my brother, which made me realize how much my father had wanted a son. I was sure he preferred Bill to me, and from then on, there wasn't anything I wouldn't do to please him and prove I was better than my brother, this despite the fact that my mother continued to make me feel very special.

My most exciting assignment was to go up in a Bell Laboratory plane and make the first radiotelephone call from the air. The purpose of the flight, according to radio engineer John Gregg, who made the historic flight with me, was to publicize the fact that Western Electric hoped in the near future to dispatch planes and bring them in by radiotelephone from the ground.

Mildred Gilman

The ascent was thrilling. It was my second plane ride, and flying was still a novelty for the average person in 1929. I was allowed to make three calls from the plane. First I was plugged into the *Journal* city room. Amster Spiro had forgotten he'd given me the assignment and said, "Where the hell are you?"

I said, "I am *telephoning* you from three thousand feet above New York City in a plane setting a record, remember?"

He said, "Oh, yes. Give your story to rewrite." That was the department that would write the story I phoned in.

I told the rewrite man breathlessly, "I am *telephoning* you from three thousand feet above New York City!"

He said, "Yeah? What's the story?"

There were two more calls. I thought I would surprise my mother in Grand Rapids, Michigan. So I called her. We connected instantly, as if she were in the next room. My voice was quivering. I could hardly get out, "Mother, this is your daughter calling you from high in the air—three thousand . . ."

She said, "I don't know who this is, but I don't think it is very kind of you." She slammed down the receiver.

That left me with one more call. At that time I was half engaged to Robert, who's now my husband; "an understanding," as it was called in those days. He was a popular, dashing young character, with all kinds of gals on the string, one in particular named Josephine. He had told the rest of them about me, but said he ought to see Josephine and tell her in person. I said, "Oh, why don't you just call her up?" I thought I'd convinced him that was the thing to do.

PART ONE

He was visiting his parents in Spring Lake, New Jersey, for the weekend. The day of the flight was Friday, so I called him. All I managed of my thrilling spiel was "Hello," and he said, "Oh, hello, Josephine. I have my bathing suit on. I'll be down on the beach in a minute." That was the end of my history-making telephone calls.

When we landed, there were reporters waiting for us on the ground, tipped off by Western Electric. One of them told Walter Winchell, the columnist, what had happened. He wrote that I had been stood up higher than anybody in history, setting two records that day. That was the end of Josephine—as a rival.

Most of the time I functioned as a sob sister, a reporter who almost literally sobbed with the victim, the culprit, the families of both, one who tried to understand why the crime had been committed, what motivated it, what sad past pressures caused the culprit to break—the mother to desert her child, the lover to slay his girlfriend, the devoted brilliant husband and father to murder a woman he had married bigamously and try to burn her body.

I was particularly sympathetic with the family of an elderly, well-educated torch murderer, Henry Colin Close. A torch murderer was one who killed someone and then set fire to the body, hoping to hide evidence of the crime. He was in dire financial straits, and to save the family he dearly loved, he had murdered Mildred Mowry. He had made her his mail-order "bride" and murdered her when she discovered his real identity and threatened to tell his legal wife.

His wife and three little girls were expecting him home for dinner in Elizabeth, New Jersey, when we reporters descended on her and told her the terrible news. I beat my way back to her apartment after the gang of reporters had left and convinced her I could help if she would let me in —and keep the others out. She agreed, and I spent two days and a night helping her with the children, protecting her against the press, and phoning my very sympathetic story to the *Journal*. She even told the officer who came to oust me at the request of the other reporters that I was a nurse and indispensable.

I grew very fond of Mrs. Close, who had believed she was Mrs. Campbell, the name her husband had assumed to hide his past. I worked with her during the long days of the trial and was with her when her husband was condemned to the electric chair. By that time I had developed a vicarious fondness for him as well and believed I understood what had motivated the terrible deed.

The only assignment I ever turned down for the paper was to witness his electrocution. I pretended to be ill, and would have been had they forced me to watch Henry Close being killed. Instead I concealed the whereabouts of Mrs. Close so no one could get near her and the children, and allowed her to have the ashes of her husband sent to my apartment from the Trenton Crematorium, again so no one could find her. Unfortunately, I forgot to mention this to my husband, and the ashes arrived plainly marked in a lead box, express charges collect, in my absence—to his shocked surprise.

Most of the time I had a lot of self-confidence, probably thanks to my mother. Also, I could look appealingly innocent and play the dumb blonde type when the occasion required it. Furthermore, I had no scruples about saying I was from the *New York Times* when admitting I worked for

PART ONE

the *Journal* would have kept me out of a highly respectable place. All this helped me to get many exclusive stories and endeared me to my boss. He was horrified when, at the top of my success, I suddenly decided to resign.

I had gotten my job in the first place by a fluke, and I left it the same way. Robert decided the tension and the fast pace, the state of being in readiness night or day to be sent on an out-of-town story were killing me, and they probably were. It was a thrilling but dreadfully hard life. What finally convinced Robert he had to do something drastic to make me quit was the self-styled Three-X murderer.

The Three-X murderer would write the *Journal* in advance, telling about a murder he planned to commit, giving the approximate location. No one believed him the first time. After his first victim's body was found, all of us were on the alert when he wrote the time and place of his second murder. I was ordered to go to College Point, Long Island, which was to be the scene of the third murder, and sit in a parked car in a wooded area at night with a *Journal* photographer. Even though Three-X had spared the first two women in the parked cars and killed only the men, Robert said, "This is too much."

After that night, Three-X wrote that he saw us all, but the woods were too lively and he had to postpone his killing. He taunted the police and wrote that the tall blonde on his list of people to be killed, "Miss Gilmore," was to be spared. Since he had mentioned my by-lined stories in his letters to the *Journal*, I felt happy to know this.

Robert had a friend in Brooklyn who was a premed student. "I am going to take you to a doctor for a checkup," he said. "At least have your blood pressure taken."

Mildred Gilman

So we went to Brooklyn, and I thought it was kind of the doctor to examine me at his home instead of his office. He frowned at my blood pressure reading and said, "If you stay on the *Journal* another month I won't be responsible for your still being alive. Your blood pressure is dangerously low." Actually it was normal, but he scared me so much that I resigned tearfully, telling my boss he would have a dead sob sister on his hands if I didn't. I had been working at top form for three years, and another three might well have killed me.

At first I worried that marriage and not having a steady good job would end my career or at least put a serious dent in it. Both Robert and I left our well-paying newspaper jobs at the depths of the depression and lived for a year on the estate of generous friends, Colonel and Mrs. Joel Spingarn, near Amenia, New York. That year I wrote the novel *Sob Sister*, among other things, and sold it to the movies. With the movie money we bought our eighteenth century house in Ridgefield, Connecticut, where we still live. One could buy a fine house and good acreage in those depression years with movie money that seems like such a small amount today.

I didn't give up journalism. I wrote steadily for *The New Yorker*, H. L. Mencken's *American Mercury*, and *Reader's Digest*. I wrote a series of short stories for *McCall's*, some of which were made into "Kraft Music Hall" stories for TV. Having written a story for the North German Lloyd's *Seven Seas* magazine, I had a free passage to Germany and return that I hated to waste. (The North German Lloyd was the most important steamship company in Germany, and *Seven Seas* was the company magazine.) Besides, I was curious

PART ONE

about the Nazi regime after Hitler had been in power one year. By this time I had two of my three sons. I found a good motherly woman to run the house and care for the family, and Robert was most understanding. It was wonderful to walk out on all the household chores.

I was almost sent as a prisoner to Dachau concentration camp because of some of my journalistic activities. The Gestapo knew I had spent an hour in Berlin interviewing Hermann Göring in the company of his constant companion, a nine-month-old lioness, asked him embarrassing questions about the regime, spent four days and nights at a women's work camp where pro-Nazi women came voluntarily to farm and to breed babies for the Third Reich, and talked with a prisoner recently released from Dachau. He had told me of the horrors already being perpetrated there. Besides, in the Munich Brown House, the Gestapo headquarters where I had applied for a pass to visit Dachau, I remarked that their huge wall map showing locations of concentration camps listed twice as many as the map I had been given in Berlin.

The Gestapo agents, after examining all my possessions and taking all my writing with them, told me to leave the country as soon as possible. My hosts were chided for taking me in. They were not Jewish and had no political connections, so no harm came to them, but at any rate they left Germany for America shortly thereafter.

In the early morning as I headed for the first train to Berlin, there were fully armed soldiers marching through the streets, preparing for a war nobody outside Germany believed possible. A man who was obviously trailing me accommodatingly helped me with my luggage, sat across from me on the train, and followed me to the home of an American friend in Berlin—all without saying a word.

Later, everyone's luggage except mine was inspected. No one opened my handbag to see how much cash I had. I thought, "Well, they aren't going to let me get to America alive, so why bother?" I had a letter from the American ambassador, William E. Dodd, in Berlin, informing Captain Zeigenbaum of the U.S.S. *Bremen* that I was getting on his ship in good condition and that they expected me to land in America in the same condition. The captain's secretary watched over me for most of the voyage home. My cabin was in tourist quarters, but I spent most of my time in first class to make the secretary's vigil easier for her. The week before, a freelance reporter from London had disappeared on the Channel crossing home. The Nazis hadn't liked what he had written.

When the *Bremen* arrived in New York Harbor, reporters were at the dock to interview Americans returning from Germany. Before I had a chance to talk with them, a rigidly erect gentleman appeared beside me. I didn't know until later that he was Captain Menzing, famous for having sunk many of our submarines during World War I, that he was living in Bronxville, New York, or that he would later be identified as a spy. "How are your friends in Munich, the von Recklinghausens?" he asked me. I said they had been fine when I stayed with them in Munich. I got the message that I should keep quiet, and I didn't tell any of my adventures to the press.

Later when the friends were safely out of Germany, I wrote articles about Göring, about the open rearming in Germany, about the infamous concentration camps, about

PART ONE

attending a Nazi storm troopers' ball, and about being sent home by the Gestapo. Only *The New Yorker* and *The New Republic* were interested in my articles damaging to the Nazis and printed many of them. *Redbook* bought a story about a young Nazi I met on the crossing to Europe; he had been ejected from the United States. They paid me five hundred dollars, a good sum for those days, and announced the story enthusiastically a month before it was to appear. It was never published, and I was told later that the business department objected because many of their advertisers were still doing business with Hitler.

After that, I spent a short interlude with the *Washington* (D.C.) *Herald* as one of Eleanor Roosevelt's "girls." My husband was working in Washington for the government at the time. Newspaper women, like generals, never really retire. My mother would be happy to know that I am still writing. Her early training has paid off.

CHAPTER 5

Norma Abrams —
Reporting for a Tabloid

The popularity of tabloid newspapers in the early twentieth century was a boon to women reporters. Tabloids, which are small newspapers the size of those often sold in supermarkets today, were filled with the lively, sensational stories that women were felt to be particularly good at. Women's careers were enhanced as a result, even for those who weren't considered sob sisters.

The New York Daily News, *where Norma Abrams worked for forty-five years, was the first tabloid. Abrams started working there in 1929 when the paper was only ten years old. Today it has one of the largest circulations of any newspaper in the country. Like most tabloids, the* News *was interested in crimes, trials, and celebrities. Divorce was much less common than it is today and often made front-page news. More space was given to local than to international news, and photographs were used in abundance.*

Abrams tells how she delayed her marriage to a fellow reporter in order to get a photograph of noted underworld figure Jack Diamond for the Daily News. *She got another scoop, beating the other reporters into print, when German saboteurs landed on Long Island, New York, at the beginning of World War II.*

She developed good news sources at the Federal Bureau of Investigation, which was a great asset when courts became her beat,

PART ONE

or specialty. Her "in" with the FBI proved especially helpful to her as the influence of organized crime spread. Abrams enjoyed covering crimes and courts more than probing other people's personal lives. She didn't like asking questions that she felt were none of her business, although she asked them when an assignment required it.

Norma Abrams retired from the Daily News *when she was eighty-one. One of the advantages of her newspaper guild contract, she said, was being allowed to work that long.*

In the Puget Sound area of Washington state, there were millions of Scandinavian churches. My first assignment on a paper in Bellingham, Washington, was to find out how many of these Scandinavian churches there were in Bellingham and how big they were. I'm sure the managing editor who gave me the assignment thought I'd go away after that and leave him alone.

Instead, I worked like a beaver. Eventually I handed him all these figures. Years later I said, "You were just trying to get rid of me. I know that."

He said, "No, no, no, no. I don't remember just why, but at the moment I wanted to know that." He didn't care a hoot about it. This was just busywork to get rid of a new reporter he didn't want very much. You see, women weren't very welcome in the newspaper business then.

I had worked at several different newspaper jobs and at one point I was working at a movie studio in Los Angeles. I was getting tired of my job in the publicity department at Columbia Pictures when some friends of mine came through town in a private railroad car and said, "We have room for you. Come on." So I joined up and came out East. Getting a job in New York in those days was pretty rough for a woman. It was not easy. First you had to get your foot in the door, which was not the easiest thing in the world to do. So you'd sort of warn people. You'd send telegrams and write letters saying that you were coming in to see them at such and such a time. If they were curious enough, they would see you. Well, I finally got a job with the *New York Daily News*. The *Daily News* was a very young paper, and it was a picture paper, with loads of photographs.

One of my first assignments after I went to work on the *Daily News* in 1929 was to cover the Morrow house in Englewood, New Jersey, in order to report on the Lindbergh-Morrow wedding. All the reporters were waiting for Charles Lindbergh and Anne Morrow to be married. His solo flight across the Atlantic had made him a national hero, so this wedding was getting a lot of attention.

Covering the wedding was almost a twenty-four-hour-a-day job. I lived in a rented car for six weeks, waiting for the wedding. We had no idea what the exact date would be. People would go in and out of the Morrow house, but nobody would talk to the reporters. I had once worked at the *San Francisco Chronicle,* where they pinched pennies, and at the *Daily News* I achieved a thousand-dollar rental car bill in the first month! It was a lot of money. I fully expected the heavens to fall, but they took it right in their stride. They did want to know if I had lived in the car, and I said, yes, I had.

The day of the wedding, Senator Morrow, Anne Morrow's father, came down to the gate to tell everybody that the couple had been married. We almost murdered each other getting to a telephone, only to find out that Lind-

PART ONE

bergh himself had called all the papers before we knew about it. He didn't like the press. I was assigned to cover the Morrow home again several years later, after the Lindberghs' baby was kidnapped.

When I started work at the *News*, it was at the time when liquor was contraband and the underworld was engaged in the bootleg liquor business. The underworld was a little different then. There were rival mobs among the Irish and the Jews instead of among the Italians as it is now. One of the important underworld figures was Jack Diamond. He had been shot and wounded and was in an Albany hospital about the time my husband and I had planned to be married. We wanted a quiet wedding because we were in no mood to take the ragging that goes on in newspaper offices. Everything was all planned, and we were going to be married in Long Island City, New York. My husband had gone out to Long Island City to make the arrangements.

I was called over to the city desk, and the city editor said, "Take the eleven o'clock train this morning to Albany and get an interview with Diamond."

I opened my mouth to say, "I can't. I'm going to be married," then quietly closed it again. I went over and got on the train, and got what turned out to be one of my biggest scoops. My husband came back to the newspaper office and thought he was shy a bride! We were married in Albany ten days later while I was still there.

In the meantime, I had talked to Diamond's lawyer. He talked to Diamond, who was short on money. Diamond had agreed to pose for pictures for the *News* exclusively. We had a bad day on that because there was static from the state police about letting us take them. But it was done, finally. The photographer took a picture and rushed back to New York with it. We were to pay Diamond five hundred dollars for posing for the picture, cash in hand. I didn't have any cash in hand because I didn't even have a suitcase. So I went down to the manager of the hotel and told him who I was. I told him I was sorry I was in his hotel with no money, but please, would he lend me five hundred dollars, and the *Daily News* would get it back to him the next day. And he did.

I never talked to Diamond. We just got the picture. We were a picture newspaper, and no one else had a picture. We would have paid him a thousand if he'd posed with his girl friend. In those days, if you had to pay to get a picture, you did.

During the arrest of Bruno Hauptmann in connection with the Lindbergh kidnapping, I had my first contact with J. Edgar Hoover, then the director of the FBI. We became lifelong friends. As the years went on, I developed a relationship of rather implicit trust with the FBI. It was a great advantage and a great time-saver in getting information I needed. As organized crime became more and more important, I had sources I could call. Often I could solve my problems with a single telephone call.

I had a city editor I trusted completely. I never hesitated to tell him what I was doing or what I hoped to do or what I knew of what the FBI was doing. There were very few things I knew that he didn't know, but there were lots of things we didn't tell anybody else. I will tell you one

PART ONE

funny story, though. This was when the German saboteurs landed on Long Island at the beginning of World War II. At that time, I would make daily calls on an FBI contact in New York who was a friend.

I was in his office one day, and as I got up to leave, he said something to me. He picked up his telephone and started to talk. I walked toward the door of his office, and as I got to the door, it dawned on me what he'd said—that German saboteurs had landed on Long Island the night before. I turned around and went back. I waited until he got off the phone and said, "What did you say?" And that was it.

He said, "Where are you going to be tonight? We're going to make an announcement tonight. We've already picked up some of them, and as soon as the last one's arrested, we're going to make an announcement."

I went to the *Daily News* office and told the city editor that I trusted the account of what had happened. We sat and waited for a call. Six o'clock came, and no call. The city editor came over and said, "You'll have to figure this out on your own. I'm going home." So I sat down and wrote a flash lead, which is a first brief news report, for the first edition. I put the lead in an envelope, sealed it, locked my desk, and went home.

My husband was at home, and he had a guest for dinner. I sat in a corner and sort of tapped my toe. I didn't have my mind on the guest or my husband, either one. Finally, in the middle of dinner, the telephone rang: I was to be down at the United States Courthouse in twenty minutes. That was a fast trip!

After the announcement at the courthouse, telephones

were made available. I knew people were listening, so when I talked over the telephone, I told the *News* exactly where I had put the flash lead, and we beat everybody into print. It was fun.

I suppose the quality that would help in the newspaper business more than anything else is trustworthiness. You have to establish a relationship of trust with the people you're talking to. If you can't inspire trust, you're all through. You need sincerity and a certain amount of diplomacy and sympathy. The thing I always had to overcome was an innate shyness. Prying into other people's lives and more intimate affairs was always very difficult for me to do. It became something I could do, but it never was easy. I think that was why I was much happier in later years when I drifted into covering courts and crime, and I didn't have to do that any more. I didn't have to go to people and say, "Why are you leaving your husband?" I never thought it was any of my business, really, why they were leaving their husbands. But it was my job to find out if I could.

The *Daily News* had a small staff in those days and a small office. You did what came your way. Everyone did some rewriting. Because we had a very early edition, the *Daily News* built up a brilliant rewrite staff. Many of them became well-known writers. Sometimes you'd write your own story, but if there was any time pressure, you telephoned it in for another reporter to rewrite. Often it was impossible to cover a story and get back to the office and write it yourself in time to get it into the paper.

Irene Kuhn was among the other women at the *News*. The *News* at that time had a great many more women than

PART ONE

any other paper in town. They were more liberal in hiring women. The *Daily News* was an equal-opportunity paper—except for money! We had experiences on the job, not so much because we were women, but because we represented the *Daily News*. Once you got past that, you had no problem. If you said you were from the *Daily News*, you might very well find yourself outside at any minute.

For example, I once covered a divorce case of some kind, which was a much bigger event in those days than it is today, especially when someone important was involved. Well, I went to ask a lawyer about his client's divorce. At that time, I owned a mink coat. I guess that's the reason I got in. Nobody stopped me, because reporters usually didn't come in in mink coats. But it was a cold day and it was snowing. It seemed like the time to wear it. I got all the way into the lawyer's office. It was a lovely office with an open fire in the fireplace. I explained to him that I had come to find out what I could about his client's divorce and that I would like a little information. He just sat and looked at me. Then he said, "You know, young woman, if you keep going out in the rain and snow like this with no rubbers, you are certainly going to get pneumonia. Good morning." That was the end of the "interview." We ran it the next morning, just like that. Since I couldn't get an interview, I wrote about that incident.

I always felt I was terribly lucky because I could earn a living doing something I enjoyed. I was having fun. Occasionally I'd make a little history as I went along, and that was just velvet.

Part Two

CHAPTER 6

Sonia Tomara —
War Correspondent

Sonia Tomara was born in 1897 in St. Petersburg, Russia, into an old, aristocratic Russian family. Her father, a Russian leftist, was highly educated and tutored her at home until the year before she entered the University of Moscow. As was typical for children of privileged families, Tomara learned several foreign languages along with her native Russian. This knowledge was important to her later when she became a war correspondent.

Tomara, her mother, and her two sisters fled Russia when the Bolsheviks became powerful. Her father stayed behind, and they never saw him again. The Tomara women went to Paris where Sonia, with almost no money, soon found work on a French newspaper.

Several years later she went to work in the Paris bureau of the New York Herald Tribune. Tomara, along with many others, had to flee again before the Germans invaded Paris in World War II because she feared she might be put in a concentration camp. She had an assignment to write a story about the exodus from Paris, so she left the car she and her sister were riding in to find a censor and a "wireless," or telegraph machine. (The censor's job during wartime was to protect national security.) She had to hurry before the censor fled, because the story couldn't be sent out on the wireless

PART TWO

until it had been censored. She tore pages out of her typewriter as fast as she typed them and gave them to the censor without even reading them.

The exodus was so chaotic and frantic, with thousands of people leaving Paris, that Tomara couldn't find another ride. She knew that she had to go back to the place where she'd left her sister or she might never find her again, so she started walking. A French soldier finally took pity on her and stopped a car for her to ride in. She managed to find her sister, and her story made the front page of the Herald Tribune.

Tomara first came to the United States in 1938 to write for the Herald Tribune in New York. She traveled by ship as there were no transatlantic flights at that time. After having covered Mussolini's Ethiopian war, the coronation of King George VI of England, the Duke of Windsor's marriage to Mrs. Wallis Simpson, and many other major political stories in Europe, Tomara's first assignment in this country was to cover a cat show. "It was amusing, but slightly humiliating!" she said with a smile. "However, it taught me about reporting in New York City."

Emma Bugbee and Kathleen McLaughlin were among the reporters who befriended Tomara during her first weeks in this country. Again, she worked her way up to covering politics, writing about foreign affairs for the Sunday edition and the editorial page and going abroad to report on the invasions of Poland and the Balkans. She finally was accredited by the War Department to go to the China-Burma-India theater after the bombing of Pearl Harbor. "You have to be interested in a story to make it good," Tomara said, and she was interested mainly in politics and international affairs.

From the China-Burma-India theater, Sonia Tomara went to Cairo, where Roosevelt, Churchill, and Chiang Kai-shek were meet-

Sonia Tomara

ing and later wrote about Roosevelt and Churchill's meeting with Stalin in Teheran. She spent six months in Algiers at the Allied headquarters there.

In the summer of 1944, after the Allied landing in Normandy, she drove in a weapons carrier into Paris where she had lived for so long before coming to the United States. It was a glorious day when she reentered Paris. She was reunited with her mother and sisters and celebrated with the throngs of people drinking champagne at the Ritz Hotel, which the Gestapo had occupied shortly before. After a winter in Paris and in Alsace with the Seventh U.S. Army, Tomara returned to New York and resigned from the Herald Tribune *to marry Federal Judge William Clark, whom she had met in Algiers.*

Here she describes some of her adventures covering the China-Burma-India theater, including what it was like to fly on a bombing mission and to share an oxygen mask with the bombardier.

Being a woman and a foreigner, I was slow in advancing as a foreign correspondent. I began as a secretary to the foreign editor of *Le Matin*, the French newspaper, in Paris. I knew languages, and that was very useful to him. I know English, Russian, and French well and can write in these languages. I know German less well, and learned some Italian when I worked in Italy. When you know several languages, you acquire others easily. Gradually, gradually, I began to write in English. I had to learn a great deal. I was lucky to have had very good chiefs at the beginning of my career.

After several years at *Le Matin*, I went over to the Paris bureau of the *New York Herald Tribune*. Leland Stowe was my chief there, and I learned a lot from him about how to

PART TWO

write a story. I worked with him from 1927 until he left to go back home to the United States in 1935. See, it was a long time, a long training. I suppose I was ambitious. I had to earn not only my living, but the living of my mother and sister. My mother was old; my sister was not as well equipped for a job as I was.

In August, 1942, I got accreditation as a war correspondent. The *Herald Tribune*, mainly Helen Reid, the publisher's wife, helped me. And I was persevering in trying to go. I was one of the first women war correspondents accredited. I had to have a uniform, and there were no women's uniforms at that time! You know, as war correspondents, we were assimilated to the rank of captain. If we were made prisoners, we were supposed to receive the salary of a captain.

I was assigned to India for about a year and a half during World War II and covered the political and military situation there and in China. I arrived in India on Coconut Day, which is about August twenty-fifth. (There are no exact days in the Indian lunar calendar.) Once a British governor of Ceylon asked me how I, a woman, got to India. I said, "I was like the British. I didn't know when I was licked!"

Not much was happening on the war front in India except in the air. The leaders of the Congress Party there —Gandhi and Nehru and their aides—were in jail; the British had taken over and dismissed the Congress. I had a fascinating time in India because I was the only woman correspondent there. I was well-known to all the fliers and had an easy time getting around because of that. I traveled all over India by air and train and saw almost everything.

Sonia Tomara

At first I could travel without any travel orders or special permissions. Then they clamped down on me! But the first time I wanted to go to our bases in Assam, I just went to the airport in Calcutta and asked if they would take me. They said, "Yeah, we'll phone you when we have a plane."

Well, they called me the next morning. We actually flew to China at about seventeen thousand feet, without any oxygen, over the Himalaya Mountains. When we stopped for the night at an air base, they didn't know where to put me. There was a hostel for men, but no facilities for women. I found an American officer who had been working on a tea plantation there before the war. The British head of the plantation and the American took me in.

A few months later, Christmas, 1942, I was in Calcutta when the Japanese bombed it. A couple of British correspondents and an Australian were staying in the same hotel that I was in when the city was bombed. The "untouchables," members of the lowest caste in India, had the job of collecting garbage. They fled from the town after the bombing, so there were mountains of garbage piling up there for days.

Then, in May of 1943, I went to China for about three months. We traveled down the Yangtze River. I was the only woman again. We were about ten correspondents—British, American, Chinese—on the ship. It was a small ship and terribly uncomfortable. It was full of bedbugs and cockroaches.

I wanted to fly on a bombing mission. The male correspondents were all flying on them, but General Stilwell, who was the commanding general of the China-Burma-India theater, said to me once, "Lady, you will not go on

PART TWO

a mission. Period." Yet I liked the man very much. He was straightforward. He met us in conferences, trusting us that the conference would be off the record and that we wouldn't print what he said. When somebody trusts you, you don't betray his trust.

I was leaving Chungking to go to Kunming to General Chennault's headquarters. I knew Stilwell quite well by that time. Being the only woman in a "man's world," you attract attention. Everybody knows you. I also knew General Stilwell's son, Colonel Joe Stilwell, who took me to his father to say good-bye. And I said, "Well, General Stilwell, do you still object to my flying on a mission?"

He said, "Well, we'll see about that." He didn't say, "No. Period."

So I decided, "Well, I can do it." I went to Chennault, and Chennault said, "You're an accredited war correspondent. Why shouldn't you go?"

So I went to Kweilin. We had a base there for B-25s, which are medium-sized bombers, and I was put on one of them. You crawl on your belly through to the front of the plane. We flew at about twenty-one thousand feet, which is pretty high without oxygen. There was a bombardier with me, and we had one oxygen mask between us. I took a few puffs and passed it on to him, and then he to me! We flew over Hankow, a big Chinese city where a Japanese military base was located. But we didn't meet our B-24s, the bigger American planes that we were supposed to meet. They flew ahead of us and were attacked by the Japanese Zeroes, their fighter planes. One of our B-24s was downed.

We had very few planes in that theater. It was pathetic, really. The loss of a plane was a tragedy. We had to bring everything over the hump, as the Himalaya Mountains were called, by plane—gasoline, bombs, the planes themselves, and everything else.

By the time the plane I was in arrived over Hankow, the Zeroes had gone away after having attacked the B-24s. So we had practically no opposition. A couple of Zeroes flew up, but they didn't catch us. We were flying in a formation of several planes, as cranes fly. We dropped our bombs, whether accurately or not, no one knows. From a height of twenty-one thousand feet, you don't see very much! But it was quite exciting.

After we dropped our bombs, we hurried south across the Yangtze River. We had the cover of some fighter planes, at least. We flew back to Kweilin, and there we learned that the B-24s had had a very bad loss. I wrote about that mission. And our public relations officer in Chungking was very angry because I had flown on a mission. He reported to Stilwell and ordered me to come to Chungking to be disaccredited, I think.

So I flew to Chungking and asked to see General Stilwell. Well, he was busy. I wrote him a letter saying that I didn't want to disobey orders, but that I thought he wouldn't mind if I flew. He wrote back a very nice note saying, "We like you and it's all right." Later when I went to Cairo, Egypt, the general in charge of our troops on the Burma border gave me a letter for the commanding general in Cairo. The letter said, "Sonia's never been in our hair. You can trust her," or something like that. I never demanded anything for being a woman or expected to have any preference over men. I was doing my work as any man would have done. I didn't see why I should ask for more.

PART TWO

During the war, it was easy because many men had been called to the colors. Women had an advantage in journalism then.

I had a lot of friends in the press corps, and of course in the faraway theater I was in, foreign and war correspondents became friends. We were like a family and tried to help each other. Sometimes if you had a special story, you wouldn't tell your competition. But for routine stories, we did exchange news a great deal.

I never tried to have scoops, because a scoop lives one day and dies the next. Newspaper articles last only one day. You don't have to have any illusions about that. I think it's more important to cover the events behind the scene rather than the obvious, which everybody covers. Any foreign correspondent for a serious paper wants to cover history, or at least have the illusion that he or she covers history.

CHAPTER 7

Irene Corbally Kuhn –
Radio Journalist and War Correspondent

Irene Corbally Kuhn's career grew right along with radio. When she was starting out in the late twenties, radio broadcasting was in its infancy. Her early broadcasts in China were made from a room covered with bed sheets for soundproofing. Because broadcasting equipment was still so primitive, she made a routine request for any listeners to call in or write that they had heard her news report.

Later, Mrs. Kuhn made the first radio broadcast from Shanghai after that city was liberated by the Allies in 1945, and also the first from liberated Manila. She has lived all over the world as a foreign correspondent and traveling journalist.

Early in her career, Irene Kuhn was fashion editor for the Paris edition of the Chicago Tribune. She has written several thousand columns of comment on the news and international politics for King Features, Columbia Features, and a third syndicate, General Features. She wrote a book about her experiences titled Assigned to Adventure and another, The Enemy Within, the first book

PART TWO

on the Communist takeover of Mainland China. The Enemy Within *is an account of Father Raymond J. deJaegher's experiences in dealing with the Communists and helping the Chinese people after twenty years of living among them in the interior, where foreigners rarely ventured.*

The Newswomen's Club of New York presented its Front Page award to Irene Kuhn in 1977 for her article on Greenwich Village in Gourmet *magazine. She is a native New Yorker and the third generation of her family to live in Greenwich Village. She still lives in the apartment where her daughter was listening to the radio one night in September, 1945, and was astonished to hear her mother's voice: "This is Irene Corbally Kuhn, broadcasting from the U.S.S., Rocky Mount, the communications ship of the Seventh Fleet, in Shanghai Harbor. . . ."*

My family was very conservative, and they did not believe in girls doing much away from home. They didn't want me going away from home at all. The only time I ever lied to my mother in my whole life was in order to persuade her to surrender my baptismal certificate, without which I couldn't get a passport. She said, "I'll give it to you if you promise to be home in six months." So I promised to be home in six months, and I didn't come home for seven years.

I went to Europe and then to China—Shanghai. I just wanted to go places. I was going to see as much of the world as I could, although I didn't know quite how I was going to do it. You didn't find one person in ten thousand who'd ever been to China. It's nothing today, but in the age of ocean liners, when we didn't yet have planes, it was quite a feather in my cap.

Irene Corbally Kuhn

About this time, in the late nineteen twenties, radio was just starting. There were missionaries with a lot of time on their hands who began to make their own little crystal sets. They were "up-country," as we called it, out of communication except by burro or by foot to the nearest village or town.

There was a fine man in Shanghai with the Kellogg Switchboard and Supply Company there. He was very busy selling parts for telephone switchboards, that sort of thing. His name was Roy De Lay. He was a very farseeing man who decided that Shanghai ought to have a radio station. He asked if I would be willing to broadcast, not for money, but just for the thrill of it. And I said, "Oh, sure." The newspaper I was working for, the *China Press*, agreed. Then he took me out into the country to see their transmitter, which was about six miles away. It was a good transmitter.

We set up a room in the *China Press* building. We stripped the room down, left the wall telephone in, brought in a mike. It was a standing mike, one of the old-fashioned ones. We hung sheets around the walls and across the ceiling to make it as soundproof as possible. Then I would go in at five minutes to six. I'd lift the telephone receiver, say hello, and hang up. This was to open the line to the transmitter. Then at six o'clock on the dot, when we were sure that the equipment had warmed up, I would start broadcasting. We didn't know whether we were being heard or not until the missionaries began coming into Shanghai from their posts up-country to report.

We had been asked by the consulates in Shanghai to send out warnings every night because rival Chinese war-

PART TWO

lords were battling each other for power, and their armies were overrunning the country. The foreigners and missionaries up-country were in real danger, and when they heard the news on their crystal sets, they began arriving in Shanghai with their families from distant areas.

Some years later, during World War II, I went back to China as a war correspondent in Chungking for NBC. But before the war, I had my own radio show when I was on the *New York World-Telegram*. I did some interesting things on that. It was a kind of feature page. I just carried that journalistic idea into radio and interviewed celebrities. Because I like things to match and come together, I used to try to find someone who was doing something or had some particular relationship to the time. On March seventeenth, for example, I interviewed Barry Fitzgerald, who was a great Irish actor.

When I joined the National Broadcasting Company in 1939, I was given the title of Assistant Director of Information; that was a public relations job. The man who hired me for NBC gave me a free rein. Whenever I had an idea, I took it to him. He was Frank Mullen, the top vice-president of the company who had taken me on originally as his assistant. So at some point, I said to him, "I'd like to go back to China and be ready to broadcast from Shanghai when the war is over." Frank Mullen was an imaginative man, and he knew from my record that I'd done some broadcasting in China in the early days. So we talked a bit, and he said, "Go ahead. Get your accreditation from the War Department and be on your way."

At first there were only two radio correspondents in Shanghai: George Moorad of Mutual Broadcasting and myself. George had come in from the Pacific Fleet. In the western district of Shanghai, there was an old school that the Germans had maintained for their children before the war. The Japanese had seized it and made it into a communications center. We inherited this, and George and a Chinese radio expert had been refining it and setting it up for broadcasting, doing all the necessary things. He had been trying to broadcast to the United States. He *was* broadcasting, but whether he was being heard, he didn't know at the time I arrived.

I used to go out every night at a certain time and try my luck, hoping somebody would hear me. When the Chinese engineer gave me the "go" signal, I'd lean into the mike and say, "This is Irene Kuhn of the National Broadcasting Company, broadcasting from Shanghai. If anyone hears me, please relay word to NBC in San Francisco." It was the most frustrating thing. It was like speaking from a vestibule into an empty apartment. But I went out in my rickshaw from my quarters in town and did it faithfully every night, sending out the news.

Then one morning I got a telephone call from a young navy lieutenant who wanted to know if I was Irene Kuhn. I said Yes. He said, "You're the NBC correspondent?"

I said, "Yes, how did you know?"

He said, "I'm calling you to present the admiral's compliments and to tell you he's bringing the communications ship of the Seventh Fleet up the river. He has asked me to extend the courtesies of the ship to you." The admiral was Admiral Thomas Kincaid, one of our best.

Well, I was just beside myself. The lieutenant said, "The admiral's been listening to you every night. There'll

PART TWO

be no problem about NBC hearing you." Of course I immediately told George. He and I went out in the admiral's gig, a small boat, and were taken down into the bowels of this big ship, the U.S.S. *Rocky Mount*. George was ecstatic and so was I. Then I thought to myself, "Well, I've blown it."

More than anything in the world I wanted to be the first person to broadcast from Shanghai, and here I was with George, a rival broadcaster. So I said, "Let's toss a coin to see who makes the first broadcast from Shanghai. That's the only fair way to do it."

He said, "You're right. You needn't have told me about this. We'll toss a coin." And then he said, "I hope you win."

I said, "George, you're great!"

So we tossed a coin, and I did win. That was how I got to make the first broadcast from liberated Shanghai. I was always glad I hadn't been a pig and kept the admiral's invitation for myself. George Moorad, a great correspondent and a fine young man, was killed a couple of years later in India. He was one of a dozen or more journalists who died in a plane crash.

The most extraordinary thing about that broadcast was that my daughter was sitting here at home in our apartment in New York. The radio was right over there where that yellow lamp is now. She was reading one night, and she had the radio on to NBC. All of a sudden she heard, "This is Irene Corbally Kuhn, broadcasting from the U.S.S. *Rocky Mount*, the communications ship of the Seventh Fleet, in Shanghai Harbor." She nearly jumped out of her skin because she hadn't heard from me recently. They had tied the broadcast into San Francisco, and San Francisco had tied it into New York. No problem. That was some ship, believe me.

It was only natural that when I returned to NBC after the Shanghai and Manila broadcasts, I should go to Frank Mullen again and say that I'd like to do some more broadcasting from New York. "Work it out with the program department and go ahead, he said. So I did. The show was called just "Irene Kuhn." It was quite successful. Then subsequently, when my daughter had been graduated from the University of Michigan, I thought it would be interesting for her to try her hand at this, see if she was interested in radio. So I conceived the idea of the first mother-daughter show, and we went on the air as "The Kuhns." We got an award, and then Mrs. Roosevelt moved in on it. Her daughter, Anna, we heard, was in dire need of money. So Mrs. Roosevelt conceived the idea of broadcasting the same kind of show. I wasn't very happy about this. How could we, or any other women, compete with that?

After the mother-daughter show, my daughter went to Europe and I shifted back to the "Irene Kuhn" show. The last one was broadcast from Spain. My daughter came over from London, and we did that show together from Madrid —and another in Spanish.

During all my working years I enjoyed what I was doing and was respected for what I did. I always had good relationships with the men I worked with. They treated me with respect and affection and generosity. The only thing that ever worried me was that I didn't get enough money, and I worked awfully hard. But then the men didn't make all that much money either.

The early days of broadcasting were a time that was

PART TWO

highly imaginative and exciting. Radio not only entertained and informed its listeners: it stimulated their imagination. But what mattered to me, in my time in broadcasting, was that I enjoyed what I was doing. I loved every minute of it.

CHAPTER 8

Carolyn Anspacher —
SAN FRANCISCO CITYSIDE REPORTER

Carolyn Anspacher was known for her style, both in her life and in her writing. She worked for the San Francisco Chronicle for nearly fifty years, starting during the depression for no salary. When she died in late 1979, the Chronicle wrote about her, "She wrote with elegance, dispatch and, often, fury. . . . The literary style could be graceful or joltingly straightforward as the situation demanded. The personal style was warm and classy."

Anspacher valued beautiful writing above all and felt that some newspaper people concentrate on their reporting at the expense of fine writing. "I'm no grubby reporter, but I'm an excellent writer," she said.

She worked hard on her reporting, though. She was trained as an actress, and her acting skills enabled her to sweep into a room and dominate it or blend in, whichever was required. Anspacher also studied the subjects she wrote about. She began studying law informally when she covered trials. Most recently, she covered the Patricia Hearst kidnapping, putting in eighteen-hour days on the average during the trial.

PART TWO

Why did she work so hard and care so deeply about her writing? "I wanted to be the very best that I could be."

I started out in life as the daughter of an extremely wealthy family. I was born in San Francisco, and my family dates way back. Buried in Home of Peace Cemetery are my parents, my grandparents, my great-grandparents, and two of my great-great-grandparents. So we're very deep in California soil!

All I ever wanted to be was an actress. I was the great star at the University of California at Berkeley. I took time out and went down to the Pasadena Community Playhouse and to the little theaters in Carmel. Everyone thought that I was going to be the new, great, young tragedienne.

Then came the depression, and this wealthy family of mine suddenly had to earn a living. Opportunities in the theater were not available for my particular type. So I sat down and thought to myself, "What can I do?" I decided out of a clear blue sky that I would be a newspaper writer. Now I'd never written a line in my life. I'd never even read newspapers, except the drama pages.

My mother knew someone who knew the publisher of the *San Francisco Chronicle*. I went in to see him, and he apparently liked me very much. He said, "What can you do?"

I said, "Everything."

So he said, "Since you can do everything and we have no staff now, we'll try you out." He took me out and introduced me to the city editor. He said, "Miss Anspacher will —maybe—fill a hole in this gaping staff." Of course, I was the only woman.

Carolyn Anspacher

The city editor said, "Now, seriously, what can you do?"

I said, "Everything." I knew I couldn't do anything. I couldn't do a bloody thing, although I could be absolutely charming at a tea table.

He said, "All right. Since you can do everything, we're going to try you out this afternoon. You will go and interview Lord Duveen. He's at the Saint Francis Hotel. He's the greatest authority in the world on Oriental jade. And he's got some of his collection with him." He added, "Our art editor is otherwise occupied."

So I phoned a friend of the family who was a big Orientalist. I went to see him before I went to see Lord Duveen, and he gave me an hour's quick course in jade. I came back and wrote a story, and the next day it carried my by-line.

To show you how long ago it was and what terrible straits the community was in, I worked for nothing for three months. The newspaper didn't have any money. Nobody had any money. They gave me expenses and thirty-five dollars a month, which they figured would cover my lunches. During that time, because of the terrible condition of the staff, they had thrown me into major stories. The first major one I did was the Lamson trial. Lamson was the head of the Stanford University Press and was charged with the murder of his wife. There were four or five trials before they decided not to proceed further. He was eventually sentenced to death, and the Supreme Court reversed that sentence.

In any event, the city editor said to me, "You will go to Palo Alto and do the running story." I didn't know a running story from a running nose. But somebody told me

PART TWO

what a running story was, which was to write the courtroom scene as it happened and have it telegraphed into the paper on yellow foolscap, page by page. I wrote it, and it was so drama-filled that the *Examiner*, which was the bigger, competing Hearst morning paper, offered me what I considered a fabulous salary, which I duly reported. The *Chronicle* met it, as they subsequently met every other offer that I've received, and there've been lots of them.

Newspaper writing became not only my bread but my wine. It was so exciting, so unpredictable, so fascinating. It offered me so much that it was impossible for me to think in terms of giving it up for the kinds of things that my generation, and the kind of conventional Jewish family in which I was reared, expected of a girl. I was supposed to get married and have children. I never did either, but I had one hell of a life.

Until the day they died, I took care of my mother and grandmother, with whom I lived in total and complete harmony. We had a large apartment, and I had my own quarters. My Victorian grandmother, who died at eighty-seven, was one of the great intellectuals of her day and was an early suffragist. She couldn't have been more pleased that I was a careerist. My mother and my grandmother delighted me. They never interfered with me, and I lived the kind of life that I wanted to live.

There was not a great story anywhere that I didn't have. I was lucky as the devil. I am still so starstruck and so beguiled by the entire concept of journalism that even writing obituaries or weather ears, the small boxes with weather reports that appear on the front page, I consider no chore. I don't mind anything.

Carolyn Anspacher

I do get terribly mad at injustice. I'm usually on the side of the underprivileged, almost always. I have won all kinds of awards for my work in mental health and retardation. The American Psychological Association and all the state mental health associations have given me awards for my work with the state mental hospitals. When Mr. Reagan was governor and had chopped the budget for these hospitals in half, I was so appalled that I did a series of pieces and never let the subject go. Reagan was forced to revamp the budget. He never forgave me, and I consider that one of the great compliments of my life.

I always figured that because I was a woman in a man's world—and for endless years I was always the only woman—I had to work twice as hard and produce twice as much as a man. I never asked to have time off to have my hair done. If I had teeth to be fixed, it was at seven-thirty in the morning. I never asked any quarter of anybody. The only thing I couldn't do was change a typewriter ribbon. That I couldn't do. I have no talent for that kind of thing at all. So someone always had to change my typewriter ribbon.

I've encountered some hostilities from my male colleagues, which I have tried very hard to overcome by letting them know that I don't want anything of them or from them and will work as hard as or harder than they. There was a lot of discrimination. When I've gotten breaks on stories, the opposing reporters have sometimes been very disagreeable and made complaints that I've used sex, or position, or quote, elegance, unquote, to defeat them. But I've almost never known a newspaperman I didn't like.

I've never had a man who was a *colleague* who did anything but try to help me. My education has come from men.

Sonia Tomara in her war correspondent's uniform. She was one of the first women to receive accreditation as a war correspondent, and there were no women's uniforms at that time.

Reproduction of a newspaper photo of Sonia Tomara.

Sonia Tomara Clark at her home in Princeton, New Jersey, in 1976.

JEAN E. COLLINS

Irene Kuhn, as fashion editor for the Paris edition of the *Chicago Tribune,* covering the major couture establishments in Paris in the 1920s.

ALLIANCE FILM SERVICE

Hazel Garland, editor-in-chief of the *New Pittsburgh Courier.*

RALPH STEINER

CARTER DI NINO STUDIOS, INC.

Photojournalist Mary Morris in 1941. She's sitting on the edge of a diving board, holding a 3¼ × 4¼ Speed Graphic camera. Her favorite camera was a smaller one, the Rolleiflex.

PART TWO

I went into this business, as I said, green as a pea. And these older men who were frequenting the newsrooms then taught me and guided me. All my life, as I've always been, I'll be grateful to these wonderful people who wanted to help me.

I expect that I have irritated a lot of people. I don't think it has ever interfered with me to a point where I was immobilized professionally. I take criticism very well. Any editorial criticism I think I probably deserved. I'm always shocked when I get reams of letters about something, half of them berating me and half of them applauding me, to the point where I consider that I've done a balanced job only if everybody equally hates me.

When I covered the birth of the United Nations in 1945 in San Francisco, I did a daily portrait of the head of one of the delegations. The stories became a great success and were made into a book. There was no one who escaped me. I deliberately stayed away from the Arab countries because they made such a terrible point about not being in proximity with anybody with any Jewish blood.

My editor came rushing out to me one day and said, "Carolyn, why haven't you done Prince Faisal of Saudi Arabia?"

And I said, "Because he doesn't like Jews."

"Well, Carolyn, he's had his prime minister phone me, and he's desperately insulted that he isn't included."

I said, "Well, I'm not going to go and be insulted."

He said, "You're going to go, and you're going to go now."

So there arrived at the *Chronicle* the Saudi Arabian limousine complete with big flag. I was taken up to this

"Jewless" fortress on top of the Mark Hopkins Hotel. There were men in costume carrying scimitars, swords with curved blades. It was like something out of *The Arabian Nights*. And there was Prince Faisal.

He said, "Why haven't you been to see me before?"

I said, "Because you don't care for Jews and I am one."

"Well," he said, "You don't look it!"

I said, "That has nothing to do with it, your highness. However, I am here to do a story about you." I stayed for two hours and drank some tea. We had a very amicable conversation. Then I went back to the paper and wrote a portrait of Prince Faisal. I said that he was "a portrait in oil, Standard Oil." And I went on from there.

I can't think of anybody in the world I haven't met. George Bernard Shaw, the Irish playwright, was on a cruise once. His ship was docked in San Francisco overnight. But Shaw had said he would not see the press. I discussed it with my boss and said I thought he ought to be interviewed. My boss said, "How are you going to get in?"

I said, "Well, I'll make it." I put on my best hand-knitted jade green dress because Shaw was an Irishman. I climbed a Jacob's ladder up the side of the ship and crawled through his porthole. He was so astonished and so flabbergasted and so enraged that I got a perfectly marvelous interview with him. I ruined the dress, I might add.

I could go places because I was rather dramatic looking. I'm a tallish woman. I had a pretty good figure, very good legs, and an innate sense of style. So I could sweep in, in the days when it was necessary to sweep in, wearing my grandmother's sable scarf. Or I could crawl through the porthole of a ship or cover a war. I could blend in with the

PART TWO

scene or dominate it. I attribute that less to my wit and wisdom than to my very, very elegant training in the theater.

Today there are a lot of young women reporters who have talent, but they're so busy being investigators that they have forgotten that the function of a newspaper writer is to write. Very little good writing is being done on newspapers today. We're so busy competing with the radio and the tube that we don't realize our function today is interpretive. We can try to capture through words—good words, beautifully modulated words—the essence and the drama and the guts of a story, which is something that the radio and the tube can't do.

CHAPTER 9

Hazel Garland –
Newspaper Editor

Hazel Garland started work at the Pittsburgh Courier *as a stringer, when she wasn't even sure what the term meant, and rose to become editor-in-chief of the paper. (As she soon found out, a stringer supplies news to a paper from a particular geographical area and is paid only for the articles that are published.) The* Courier *was founded in 1910 and at that time was the only United States newspaper with a national circulation that was oriented to blacks. Its coverage and circulation expanded under Garland's leadership.*

The oldest of sixteen children, Garland grew up in Pennsylvania where her father was a coal miner. She had no money for college, but her education didn't stop. She kept reading, taking courses, and attending concerts and the theater, sometimes standing through a performance when she couldn't afford a seat.

At the Courier, *she reported on poverty in rural South Carolina and protested the poll tax that was charged in some states in an effort to discourage blacks from voting. She also wrote about movies and television and interviewed many stars and celebrities. Garland met Eleanor Roosevelt on several occasions when Mrs. Roosevelt invited the National Council of Negro Women to have tea at the White House. An active council member, Garland found*

PART TWO

the First Lady a "superb person, with depth of character and mind."

Hazel Garland's daughter followed in her footsteps. Phyllis Garland is a writer, specializing in music, and is an associate professor on the faculty of Columbia University's Graduate School of Journalism. It was in Phyllis Garland's New York City apartment, among wall-to-wall record albums and books, that her mother and I talked.

Now in her "retirement," Hazel Garland writes columns for the Courier *and serves as a consultant to the paper. She continues to support the need for a strong black press to report on areas where change is still needed and on issues that aren't thoroughly covered elsewhere.*

I always liked to read, and I always liked to write. But when the time came for me to think about going to college, the depression was in full swing. You could hardly *buy* a job. My father was a dear soul. I loved him dearly. But his idea was, "Why waste your money on sending a girl to college? She's going to get married. Save your money for the boys." Well, that was before women's lib! I really wanted to go to school badly.

I have a sister next to me, and a brother who was third down the line. My father worked in politics and got my brother a senatorial scholarship, but my brother was so in love with some girl that *he* wanted to get married, and he didn't take the scholarship! It made me angry because I worked, and even did day's work, helping him to get through high school. After school, I washed dishes for one of my teachers and scrubbed her kitchen floor. I ironed clothes. I did everything I could just to get a little extra money. My mother always told us that it was no disgrace to work, and whatever you do, do it well and take pride in the work you do. I bought the suit my brother was graduated in. I couldn't afford the high school ring, but I did get a high school pin for him. He gave the pin to this girl, and I never even got a chance to see it!

I used to go to the library where I would read and read. Because I wasn't going to college, I felt that I would try to do what I could to educate myself. They didn't have student loans for young people as they do today. I lived in libraries. I read everything. That's why I say there's no excuse for a person today not to take advantage of all the opportunities that are available. There's no excuse for ignorance.

I still read everything I can get my hands on, and I also like to talk to people. I've always made it a point to be around people I could learn something from. I'm constantly trying to learn something more. I figure you're never too old to learn if you keep an open mind. Don't be afraid or embarrassed to say that you don't know a thing. After all, people will find out eventually!

Because I liked to write, in every club, church, or other group I belonged to someone would always say, "Hazel, you be the club reporter." Or, "Hazel, you serve on the publicity committee." So I was on the publicity committee for the local YWCA when our first black staff worker was hired in 1943. I was to notify the different radio stations and newspapers; we didn't have television in those days.

One of the papers I notified, of course, was the *Pittsburgh Courier*. I wrote the city editor a letter and explained that something really unusual was happening in McKees-

PART TWO

port. They still had segregated Ys in Pittsburgh, and this was going to be the first Y in Allegheny County to be integrated. I called to follow up and see if the city editor had received the letter. He had and was planning to send a reporter and a photographer.

Well, we had a big tea on Sunday to welcome the new staff member. We had a nice crowd. It was a beautiful day. And we waited and waited. Some of the newspapers and radio stations had sent reporters to cover it, but no photographer. As I was waiting I said, "I hope the Negro newspaper will at least have a photographer too." (We were Negroes in those days!) As time was passing, I finally called my husband, who was just starting his photography business. I asked him to come down and take a picture. He took a picture of the new woman with the executive secretary and the president of the board. They were around the tea service. Then we had the oldest member of the board shaking hands with her.

When everything was over and everybody was leaving, a car pulled up, and a girl from the *Pittsburgh Courier* came over. She worked on Saturdays and Sundays helping the women's editor. She said, "I guess I made a mistake and went to the wrong place. I thought it was in McKees Rocks, not McKeesport." McKees Rocks was at the opposite end of Pittsburgh. I said I'd written down everything about the event. She said, "Since you've done all that, why don't you just take that information in to the women's editor? If she isn't there, give it to Wendell Smith." He was the city editor at that time.

I went in and saw the city editor, Wendell Smith, because the women's editor was out. (Wendell Smith and the late William G. Nunn, who was managing editor of the *Pittsburgh Courier*, were responsible for integrating baseball. They introduced Jackie Robinson, the black second baseman, to Branch Rickey. As a result, Jackie Robinson broke down the racial barriers in baseball.)

Wendell Smith looked over what I'd brought and said, "This is pretty good." He took me into the managing editor's office. I was shaking a bit, a little nervous. After looking over my copy, Mr. Nunn said, "You've got the facts, the information down. It could be changed around a little bit. For one thing, you can spell, and the grammar's correct. You've got the main ingredients of who, what, when, where, why." Then he said, "You live in this tri-city area of McKeesport-Clairton-Duquesne. How would you like to be a stringer?"

"A stringer?" I asked.

He said, "Yes."

I said, "Sure." I didn't know what *stringer* meant, but I figured it meant something about the paper giving me a chance to write.

I went home and told my mother-in-law, Mrs. Janey Garland, who was staying with us at the time. My daughter, Phyl, was a little girl, and I could leave my daughter with her. I said, "Oh, mother. You know what? I'm going to be a stringer for the *Courier*."

She said, "What is a stringer?"

I said, "I don't know exactly what it means."

She said, "How much do they pay?" It struck me then, I hadn't thought to ask about pay. Of course, I've never made that mistake since. I soon learned that money is very important. But at the time, I was just so interested in get-

PART TWO

ting an opportunity to write, to do something that I felt was creative.

I went back the next week, and I carried in a few news items. I said, "I've got to ask you. What does *stringer* mean?"

Wendell Smith said, "That means if something comes up in McKeesport, if some important person dies, or is appointed to a high position, if there's a fire or something, we can call you and ask you to find out about it. Since our paper is geared toward Negro readers, you might be asked to get an angle on that. If there was a fire, you'd ask if there were any Negroes in the fire. And you call in the news to us."

I said, "Well, what about the money?"

He said, "We don't pay very much, but we'll pay you two dollars for anything we print." Right away I got busy. I went around to the McKeesport, Clairton, and Duquesne city councils and introduced myself. I went down to the police station and told them that if there were any murders or anything to let me know! I sent notices to all the churches and asked for their news.

I couldn't type, so my husband rented a typewriter and I taught myself how to type. That week I carried in loads of material. Most of it went into "File Thirteen," naturally —the wastebasket. Most of it they already had. The *Courier* is a weekly newspaper. The editor explained to me that any story that is important would be carried in the dailies. After the daily newspaper carried it, you had to get a different angle to make it fresh.

Then he said, "You're working better than our regular reporters. Why don't you take a lot of this stuff and write it up in a column called 'Tri-City News'?" I said okay, and

Hazel Garland

I started my column. When I joined the staff full-time in 1946, the column was changed to "Things to Talk About." It was about club meetings and birthdays and births. People wanted to see their names in print. They started calling me or writing me with little news items. If a club was celebrating an anniversary or planning a tea, for example, I got the news. My column became very well read.

I learned a lot. Finally, I got to the point where I could write pretty well. There were a number of us writing small-town columns. They said that those of us who were interested could come into the *Courier* on Saturday mornings, and one of their editors, Ted Stanford, who had taught journalism, would be there and teach us for nothing. So I made it my business to go every Saturday. He was hard as nails!

Finally, he was made city editor. Wendell Smith was sent out to follow Jackie Robinson, and they gave his spot as city editor to Stanford. He seemed to hate women. He also felt that women had no business in news. Many times he had me in tears. I was substituting when regular reporters were on vacation or sick. One time there was a murder down in the red-light district of Pittsburgh. Stanford sent me down there to the house where the murder occurred. I was afraid to go, so I said, "Well, I . . ."

He said, "You want to work? Now if you're going to act like a man, you've got to go there and cover. That's your assignment."

There was a young fellow who covered the police beat. Mickey was always broke, so I said, "Mickey, I'll give you a dollar if you'll go into this house with me, because I'm afraid to go in alone." It was terrible. I was afraid they

PART TWO

might think I was one of the girls of the street! I wasn't bad looking. I weighed about a hundred and ten pounds and was built nicely. So I went there with Mickey, and I got the story and brought it back. Stanford was angry because I succeeded and did that story. He didn't ask me what happened, and I didn't volunteer any information.

In 1946, there was an opening for a full-time reporter on the staff. At that time we had just formed a newspaper guild. Until then, the *Courier* had been nonunion. Everyone said, "Oh, Hazel. You came down at the right time." We got the same wages that the downtown papers paid. In the meantime, I had covered everything, so they made me assistant women's editor. They later transferred me to features.

They sent me all around the country. The *Courier* was very strong at that time. We were protesting lynching. We were trying to get the poll tax abolished. During World War II, we fought for victory at home as well as victory abroad. We called it the Double V campaign. That meant we were working for racial equality at home as well as victory in the war.

We did stories on a Negro sharecropper who had shot and killed her white employer when he attacked her. We raised funds for her defense. She went to jail, but her life was spared. Our circulation soared from one hundred thousand to almost four hundred thousand readers during that period. In the larger cities, we had branch offices. We had correspondents in other cities, even in the Caribbean islands and in London and Paris.

I had an opportunity to travel everywhere. In 1952, I went to a rural area of South Carolina to do a story on an unusual black nurse-midwife, Maude Cullum. She was a registered nurse and had brought many of the children of that area, white and black, into the world.

Oh, I never cried so hard. To see such poverty! This was in January and there were children walking around with hardly any clothes, barefoot and living in houses with little doors for windows—no panes. They had little chunks of newspaper stuffed in the wall to keep out the cold. There were so many babies, and their parents didn't think about getting married. In fact, one woman said that it was a woman's *duty* to have children! I visited the schools. The children dropped out, and they had little or no education. What hope was there? So I wrote a series called "The Three *I*'s: Ignorance, Illiteracy, and Illegitimacy."

The *Courier* entered the story in a competition. Every year we had what was called a Page One Ball. All newspapers that were members of the guild sent their best material to be judged. One of the judges was from the *New York Times*, one was from the *Cleveland Plain Dealer*, and one was from the *Chicago Sun-Times*. The *Courier* was the only black newspaper among all of the newspapers in western Pennsylvania. All were dailies except ours.

The entries were numbered. They didn't name the newspaper or the reporter who wrote it, or mention whether the person was black or white. I won the award for the best series. The prize was awarded at the Page One Ball. Oh, I was so thrilled. And I was *shocked*, too, because I beat some people who had been perennial winners. One had won a Pulitzer Prize the year before and had entered a series. I said that if I don't win anything else again, I had won that.

PART TWO

I was named entertainment editor, then radio-television editor. I used to go out to Hollywood. That included covering movies and the legitimate theater, which I loved. I've interviewed just about every great black star and white star in the business. I remember years ago Rosalind Russell came to Pittsburgh in the play, *Bell, Book and Candle*. We had dinner at her suite. She was so nice. Later I met Bette Davis when she tried out a musical in Pittsburgh. When I was in Hollywood I met Humphrey Bogart, Barbara Stanwyck, Tony Curtis, Janet Leigh, Sidney Poitier. I did one of the first big feature stories on Harry Belafonte, the black singer. Whenever Belafonte came to Pittsburgh, he always got in touch with me because he said I was the first one to help him get a big break.

I always tell young people who are deciding whether to take up journalism not to expect to get rich, unless they marry the publisher of the newspaper, and how many can do that? They have to realize it's hard work. But there are many fringe benefits.

Once I did a story about a little girl who had some sort of ailment that caused her to need extra oxygen. It cost eight dollars and forty-nine cents a day, so we called her "the eight forty-nine girl." We had a special room built onto her parents' house because she had to have pure air—no germs or anything. We built this room and furnished it, and the paper paid for the oxygen until she died. When you do things like that, it makes you feel you're accomplishing something.

Around 1960, many newspapers were having problems. Many newspapers were folding. The *Courier* was having problems because the price of newsprint, the paper a newspaper is printed on, and printer's ink went up. Unions were asking for more money, and there were strikes, and so forth. Mrs. Robert L. Vann, whose husband left her the *Courier*, was a very nice person, but she wasn't a businesswoman. Some of the men took advantage of her. As a result of the high cost of operations and poor business management, checks began to bounce.

I *loved* the *Courier*. It was everything to me. I had spent the greater part of my life there, so I wanted to work even if I didn't get paid. I thought maybe we could keep on and hold it together. At the time, I was women's editor. Then, in 1965, a man who was a cosmetics manufacturer in Chicago took over. He tried to keep it going, but he knew nothing about journalism.

In 1966, I went away on my vacation for three weeks. When I came back, I learned the *Courier* had been sold to John Sengstacke of Chicago, who owned several black newspapers. The *Courier* was renamed the *New Pittsburgh Courier*. I continued as women's editor. One day Jim Lewis, the general manager, said "Sengstacke's on the phone. He wants to talk with you." Right away, I began to wonder what I had done. I figured that I must have done something wrong! So I answered the telephone.

He started talking cheerfully, so I thought it must not have been anything too bad. I was still trying to think what he was calling me about. Then he said, "You know, Hazel, we need a city editor."

I said, "You certainly do." I had been doing a lot of the work after our city editor quit because no one else knew how to lay out the pages and write heads.

He said, "Can you recommend anyone?" Being brain-

PART TWO

washed to think only of men working in news, right away I started thinking of men. I named two or three and said there weren't too many around here. But at that time, most white papers had at least one black person.

I said, "Maybe you can woo one of them away. You may have to pay him a little more than he's getting."

He said no. Everybody I recommended, he said no.

"Well," I said, "Mr. Sengstacke, just what do you want?"

He said, "First thing, I want someone who knows the community, who knows the business, someone who has had some experience in the newspaper business. I want someone who knows how to deal with people, someone who is tactful and can get along with all kinds of people, someone who can go across lines, who can deal with black and white issues and all factions, rich and poor."

He named all those things, and I said, "You know you're calling for quite a person. Just offhand, I can't think of anyone here in Pittsburgh who can fill the bill." I said, "I'll tell you what. I'm going away for two or three days because I've been working so hard, and I've delayed taking my vacation. While I'm off, I'll try to think of someone."

He said, "No, I've already made up my mind. I know someone."

In the meantime, Jim Lewis, the general manager, kept saying. "What's he saying? What's he saying?"

Then Sengstacke said, "I know someone."

I said, "Who?"

He said, "You."

I said, "*Whooo*?" And I almost dropped the receiver.

He said, "Didn't you ever think of yourself as having those qualifications?"

I said, "No, frankly I hadn't." And I said, "To tell you the truth, if you had asked me this ten years ago, I would have jumped at the chance because that is quite a challenge. But I'm getting kind of old, and I'm thinking of retiring pretty soon."

He said, "Oh, you're not that old. You don't have to retire." That was in 1972 and I was about fifty-eight. I looked younger than I do now.

I said, "You know, I'd like to think about it. Since I'm going away for a few days, give me some time."

He said, "Oh, I realize you have to have time to think. I believe in giving you all the time in the world—two minutes."

All this time, Jim Lewis kept saying, "What's he saying?"

I said, "Wait just a minute, Mr. Sengstacke." Then I said, "You know, Jim. He asked me to become city editor."

Jim said, "He asked you what?"

I said, "He asked me to be city editor."

Jim looked at me and said, "You're not going to take it, are you?"

I said, "Why not?"

He said, "Frankly, Hazel, I don't think that's a woman's job. I think being city editor belongs to a man. And your age . . ."

So I turned around and said, "Mr. Sengstacke, I accept. If you think I can do it, I'll give it a try."

He said, "If I didn't think you could do it, I wouldn't have asked you. I know you can do it. You go ahead on your

PART TWO

vacation. When you get back, we can get the money straightened out."

So I said, "Well, I want the same that you'd give a man, since you think I can fill the bill." I was looking at Jim Lewis all this time. As general manager, he was the one who was going to have to make out the paycheck.

I turned around after I hung up and said, "Jim, as you well know, I didn't ask for this job. He asked me. Now I can work with you. But if you can't work with me, then *you* better tell that man. Because I can work with the devil himself, and sometimes I think that's just what I'm doing."

He said, "Oh, we can work together, if that's the way he wants it."

I said, "Yes, that's what he said."

So I worked *hard*. I worked night and day, many times. I'd go over on Saturdays and do some things. In 1973, the next year, the circulation had gone up. We had better ads, and the paper was looking classy. I tried to organize the paper into sections. Definitions of "women's news" were changing. So I changed the women's section to the Leisure Living section and included articles about men, too. We published more features, and we had someone who covered labor.

We subscribed to many papers to see what was happening in other places: the *New York Times*, the *Washington Post*, the *Chicago Tribune*, the *Cleveland Plain Dealer*, the *St. Louis Post-Dispatch*, the *Milwaukee Journal*. We had a national edition, and we wanted to check on things going on throughout the country. One of those papers would have a story about some person, and we'd get a different angle on it. We'd want to find out what caused someone to do such a thing, what the motivation was. Maybe somebody was appointed to something. We'd want to have the black angle, the background of the person. As a result, we were able to build up our readership on the national level. In 1976, we won the National Newspaper Publishers Association John Russwurm Award, which is given to the best black-oriented newspaper in the country.

After the sixties, when there had been a lot of battles between blacks and whites, I wanted to hire a young man as copy editor. He was white. All of the best blacks were going to white newspapers, advertising agencies, public relations firms, television, and radio. Jim Lewis said, "Since we're a black newspaper, I don't think we should have any whites."

I said, "Wait a minute. We're talking about fair employment. It works both ways." I called Mr. Sengstacke and said, "Do you have any preferences as to the color of the person serving as copy editor?"

He said, "No, I don't. I don't care if he's green."

I said, "That's all I want to know." I hired the man, and he was just terrific.

I was promoted from city editor to editor-in-chief in 1974. After a couple of years, I started to have problems with blood pressure. Heart and kidney disease run in our family. So I told Mr. Sengstacke I would just have to give up my post as editor-in-chief, but that I would continue to write my column if the paper wanted me to. I'd been writing "Things to Talk About" since 1946, my commentary on people, places, and things. I also wrote a column called "Video Vignettes," about television. In May, 1977, I packed

PART TWO

up my things and went home, and I've been writing columns ever since.

I think there's still a need for a good black press because we haven't reached a utopia. There still has to be a voice. There are blacks on white papers, but they are not, with a few exceptions, given positions of authority, or the authority to cover certain things in the black community. In Pittsburgh, people are still fighting to get integrated schools. Until things are right, there has to be someone to keep prodding, to keep the public aware of the issues.

Journalists are always looking, always thinking. They're able to see that there's more than one side to anything, to any question. People who live narrow, sheltered lives miss something. My best friends have always been in the business.

CHAPTER 10

Mary Morris —
PHOTOJOURNALIST

Mary Morris was one of the first women to become a full-time newspaper photographer when she went to work for the Associated Press Feature Service in 1937. William McCleery, who hired her, said recently that she was an excellent photographer because of her ability to capture human interest in her photographs, because she had a sense of humor, and because she was able to get people to look natural. "A photographer paints a picture on people's faces, then takes the picture," he said. "She was good at evoking the right expression on a person's face and capturing it in a photograph."

If you compare Mary Morris's photographs with the news photographs of the time you will notice that hers were more like feature stories than straight news. She tried to show why things happened or what they meant; instead of one photograph, a series was often used. It was the beginning of a new technique—the story told in pictures, with captions.

Charles Norman, the reporter who worked with her most regularly at the AP, recalled in a recent memoir, "She was a first-rate photographer and a very good companion. Sometimes, when I thought her occupied with her photo equipment, she surprised me by asking a question of her own. At first this rattled me, but never

PART TWO

the person being interviewed, who may have thought it part of the procedure."

Poet Edna St. Vincent Millay wrote Norman about the photographs Morris took of her: "Before you can use the one with the hand to the head you'll have to offset the brutality of a clinically probing camera operating in the glare of full sunlight, by the handsomest job of retouching in the history of the AP. Spots, blots, freckles, speckles—everything that the camera is particularly proud of—I want wiped right out. My desire in the matter is very simple: I just want to look as pretty as possible."

Morris's job was physically demanding. She had to carry equipment to several assignments a day, always by public transport or on foot; no taxi fares were allowed on the expense account. For this reason, she wore comfortable clothes, full skirts with pockets, a shoulder-strap bag made to order (because none were available in stores at the time), and flat-heeled shoes. She remembers receiving stares when she wore trousers into Saks Fifth Avenue in the midfifties because this was not an accepted practice at the time.

Mary Morris describes in this chapter the style that characterized her work, some of the stories she covered, and her most memorable photographs.

It's nice if a photograph lasts, if it turns out to be very good and is worthwhile later on. But my job has been to tell stories and at the same time to get a couple of shots good enough to stop people when they're flipping through a magazine or newspaper. I'm not the kind of person who aims to make pictures that go on people's walls.

I have almost nothing on my walls. Well, there is one photograph of Gena Bachauer, the great pianist. She's dead now, but she was one of the world's foremost pianists. I took a picture of her in New York, where she was practicing on the Hunter College stage. In the photograph, you see the empty auditorium, the pianist silhouetted, and the figure of a man cleaning the stage floor behind her. It was dramatic: this lone woman filling the great hall with marvelous music. The only other person there was that man, mopping. That sort of thing happens all the time, but nobody ever *sees* it: a musician practicing in a huge place with no audience. That is a good shot, and it will last. It tells everything in one fast glance.

When I went to work for the Associated Press in 1937, it was unusual for a woman reporter to be hired to do general assignments. To be hired as a general assignment photographer was even more unusual. I guess there were a few other women photographers around the country on small newspapers, but none in New York. You could say I had a unique career. Few women worked on the serious side in newspapers, and those who did were told to write "the woman's angle."

Why was I hired? Well, I knew the right person—my roommate's boyfriend, William McCleery. He was head of the Feature Service at the Associated Press and thought it would be smart to have a different kind of photographer on his staff. It was daring of him to make the suggestion to the big boss, the general manager of the AP, Kent Cooper. Cooper thought McCleery was a very clever young man—McCleery was only twenty-seven—and let him have his way. I suppose I was an embarrassment to a lot of those men a lot of times. But eventually they got accustomed to having a young female around—on the newsroom floor, back in the darkrooms.

PART TWO

In those days most news photographs consisted of flash pictures. The flash was on the camera, glaring into people's startled faces, generally on a dead black background. News photographers were chosen mostly for physical stamina, ability to push through crowds, carry a heavy pack, shoot over people's heads, stand on one foot on top of a wall. That sort of thing. I was not only less rugged, but college-educated (Sarah Lawrence) and interested in people and new ideas about almost everything. Basically I've always been an activist and filled with curiosity. I suppose those are the qualities that helped to turn me into a good journalist.

I developed a style quite different from regular news photography. We at the Associated Press Feature Service and the people at *Life* and *Look* magazines, which got started a couple of years later, set a journalistic picture-story style. We were after a candid, or documentary look. So we used small cameras, available light with no flash, or flash or photoflood bulbs aimed at the walls or ceilings in what is called "bounce flash," to simulate natural light. These techniques give a realistic look to our shots, very different from studio lighting or regular news flash pictures.

AP news photographers were using four-by-five Speed Graphics with heavy wooden holders for their pieces of cut film. Most of the time I used a Rolleiflex, a much smaller camera. Three rolls of film for my camera probably weighed less than one of their film holders, which held only two pieces of film. Nowadays the Speed Graphic has all but disappeared, and news photographers have turned to the small cameras; darkrooms are mechanized and processed by machine. All very different.

At the beginning, I was sent out on stories with various male reporters, some of whom have become famous: Charles Norman, who later became a novelist, poet, and biographer, and James "Scotty" Reston, who went on to make a big name for himself at the *New York Times*, both as a political columnist and as head of the *Times* Washington bureau. Reston was working a nightclub beat, and I remember going to some seedy places with him. Both were very interesting young men with a passion for books. On the way back to the office each of them would want to steal some time visiting secondhand book shops. I loved it. We never told the boss why our assignments took so long.

When we went to interview people, everyone would do a double take when I walked in, no matter whether it was in a famous person's living room or at New York's Yankee Stadium. I understand that it was only recently that women were given free access to the stadium. But way back in the late thirties, I actually went out on the field and took pictures. I don't remember how it was arranged. Perhaps there was no opposition because there was only one of me around town and I was considered sort of a curiosity. I just remember everyone screaming and hooting and carrying on when I walked onto the field. I suppose I enjoyed it.

When I turned up at a fight training headquarters in New Jersey, I remember all those tough-looking fight types staring at me as if to say, "What? This broad with a camera?" I guess I enjoyed that too. Meanwhile, back at the office, my boss was getting a charge out of sending a woman into these places. He was not a man to do things by the rule

PART TWO

book. But he was solid too. I learned a lot from McCleery. He in turn learned a lot about what a photographer like me could produce. He went on to *Life* magazine. I've worked with a lot of talented people.

After three years with the AP, I quit to go to *PM* newspaper. It was a new tabloid paper with no advertising. The idea was that we wouldn't be influenced by advertisers. Ralph Ingersoll, who had been a big man at *The New Yorker* and then at *Time* raised the money to start this unusual paper. Nearly every newswriter in town wanted a job there. It was a sensational, young staff, most of us under thirty. Ingersoll was the oldest at forty-two, and a few of the top editors were in their thirties. It was a tremendous opportunity for us all—to start something new and original.

I was the first photographer hired at *PM*. In the end there were about fifteen of us, only one other female—Margaret Bourke-White. She quit *Life* to come to *PM*. She was already famous and a lot older than I. I covered a lot of theater and dance for *PM*. I remember a seven-page picture story on the making of a musical play, *Pal Joey*. That meant attending tryouts for the casting, sitting in the darkened theater with Dick Rodgers, the composer; Larry Hart, the lyricist; and Johnny Green, the conductor. I would listen to them discuss the people up on the stage, those poor people hitting the wrong notes, quivering with shaking knees, and so on.

It was fun watching a show being put together, going on the road with them, recording with my camera all the worry and the changes. *Pal Joey* went down in history as a musical that broke new ground; it was a serious story by

John O'Hara, with a heel as the hero. A number of my pictures were used in Richard Rodgers's autobiography, which came out a few years ago.

I slipped over into writing during World War II when some of the guys at *PM* said, "Hey, you're a better reporter than a lot of these types we've been hiring to replace people who have gone to war. We don't have to teach you how to get the story. We'll just teach you how to write." And they did. I would turn in my stories and then hang over their shoulders as they fixed the spelling, transposed the phrases, tightened the wording. That was a great way to learn. I still figure I'm a better photographer than writer, but I've written for a lot of national publications over the years.

When my first husband, Ralph Steiner, the photographer and filmmaker, went to work in Hollywood, I was allowed to become a writer-photographer for *PM*. I remained on the staff, but lived in California and started turning out stories, mostly about the film stars. Occasionally I did some political stories. Most of what I did appeared in *PM*'s Sunday magazine, so I wrote two-to three-thousand word pieces and shot pictures to go with them.

I had a daughter while I was in California, took six weeks off (with pay) when she was born, then went back to work. Since I worked from my home, the transition into the mother role was not difficult. After the war and when *PM* had folded, my first husband and I returned to New York and went into advertising photography. The studio was in our brownstone house in the East Sixties, so again combining child-raising and strenuous work was easier than if I had gone out to business daily. The big trick was

PART TWO

finding the right person to look after our child when I was occupied with the job.

Our daughter, Antonia, turned out to be a good, if not always willing, model. She was cute looking and cheaper than the professional models! She appeared in many ads, as did her friends. They liked posing for me, and it made them big in their own circle. Also they earned a little money and thought the studio atmosphere was marvelous. My studio was a drop-in place for a long time. One little boy who was about ten years old used to come in his overalls right from shop class at school. He was good with his hands and liked to help. He also liked to look at the beautiful, grown-up models.

I more or less officially retired when I moved to London with my second husband, Harold Lawrence, when he was appointed manager of the London Symphony Orchestra. I was glad of an excuse to stop earning a living! I had no work permit in England so I started giving away my services. I did quite a lot of work for musical artists and for the symphony. Traveling around the world with the orchestra, I did pictures backstage, onstage, in airplanes. Musicians and their instruments make good photographs. It's a lot easier to get something interesting from them than from your ordinary, middle-class upright citizen.

We live now in Oakland, California, where my husband is president and general manager of the Oakland Symphony Orchestra. On the walls of his office are pictures I have taken for record covers and for the various needs of the symphony orchestras he has been associated with: a picture of Leonard Bernstein walking on a curving wet path in a London park on the way back to the rehearsal hall after lunch. I'd taken my camera to lunch, but it was the unplanned walk back that got me the picture we still like to look at.

There's a shot I "stole" from a balcony overhanging the stage in Moscow showing André Previn under a huge British flag, conducting a performance with the London Symphony. There's a shot of Sir William Walton, the British composer, walking down the aisle in Leningrad being pelted with flowers, the Russian custom. I wouldn't have gotten that shot if I hadn't been sitting next to him, with my camera concealed under my purse. When he rose to take a bow after his piece had been performed, I followed him into the aisle and started shooting. No officials tried to stop me as they saw I was with Sir William, part of the act. I got a whole series of good pictures.

There's another shot from Moscow that we like, showing Previn and Walton backstage toasting each other with cans of English beer supplied by the British embassy. It's a wide-angle shot, giving a view of backstage atmosphere, of the mirrors and dressing room lights.

I don't want to go on talking about the famous people I've shot, or hung around with, from Frank Sinatra to Judy Garland to Jack Kennedy in the White House and British Prime Minister Edward Heath in residence at 10 Downing Street. Every photographer who gets anywhere spends interesting time with big shots. I worked on a series of full-page color shots for *Fortune* magazine on presidents of American corporations, and I can tell you that most of their suits didn't fit very well and that we spent a lot of time with straight pins and clothespins trying to give them a pulled-together look.

PART TWO

What I want to emphasize is not the glamour. It's that a career in photography can be rewarding, and it's tough work. The competition is a lot worse now than when I began. I came in at a good time. Photography wasn't such an obvious career then. I went to a photography school for one whole year after college and considered it a waste of time. I learned most of what I needed from my first husband, who was older than I and already an accomplished photographer.

I used to tell young people to stay out of the photography schools and attach themselves to a skilled practitioner. Now there seem to be many good schools that you can attend full-time. Or you can pick up a course here and there. The photography magazines and technical books tell you much of what you must learn. I still suggest trying to hitch onto a photographer who has a business and knows what he or she is doing. One learns the ropes that way.

There are hundreds of kinds of photographers. When I started, I never thought I'd end up doing ads. But I got into it because it paid big money and they were waiting for people like me. The artificial, stiff photos made in the studios gave way to the candid, real, journalistic approach. So I did well for many years doing ads for food, whiskey, cigarettes—the big stuff. My last ad campaign was for Camel cigarettes, with huge billboards and ads in all the national magazines. I'm glad to be out of it. It's a tough business, though I enjoyed some of it at the time. Journalism was better.

Part Three

CHAPTER **11**

Mary Garber –
Sportswriter

Mary Garber was a full-time sportswriter at a time when women reporters were almost as rare as a four-minute mile. The hurdles she faced were nowhere near the locker rooms that women sportswriters are trying to enter today. Garber had to persevere just to persuade coaches to speak with her, join a professional sportswriters' association, and sit in the press box, much less the locker room.

She has been reporting on sports as a member of the Winston-Salem *(North Carolina)* Journal *and* Sentinel *sports departments since 1944. She's written about almost every sport at some time: football, basketball, baseball, boxing, wrestling, swimming, auto racing, steeplechase, skeet shooting, golf, tennis, horse shows, track, cross-country, tennis, and the Soap Box Derby. She covers mainly college sports, often wearing sneakers and the black and gold knit cap that has become her trademark. When she's not covering a game or writing her tennis column, Garber enjoys playing tennis herself.*

She got her start on the Sentinel *in 1940 as a society editor. After about a year, she switched to the news side, covering several different beats. Garber became sports editor when the men on the*

PART THREE

staff were away during the second world war and was able to continue in sportswriting when they returned.

The Journal-Sentinel *honored her recently by establishing a Mary Garber award, which is given to the most outstanding female basketball player in Northwest North Carolina. She has won first place in national writing contests for her articles on baseball and basketball.*

Mary Garber tells here about what she has learned from sports and sportswriting, about the thrill of covering international competition, and about her regret at being closer to the end of her work than to the beginning.

We moved from Ridgewood, New Jersey, to Winston-Salem, North Carolina, when I was eight years old. Like all children, I was forced to write letters back to my grandparents, who lived in Ridgewood. Rather than write "Dear Grandma and Grandpa," I had a newspaper called the *Garber News*. I put all the family news in that, with big screamer headlines. When the dog bit the cook, I'd write that up as a news story. I was eight when I decided to go into the newspaper business, and I never at any time changed my mind.

I got into sportswriting in 1944, during the second world war. I was working on the news side of the *Winston-Salem Sentinel*. While the men were away fighting the war, a high school boy used to come by and put out the sports page before he went to school. Then he went into the navy, and there wasn't anybody to take his place. The staff was all women at that time. I'm not sure why, but I was picked to handle the sports page. I just got fascinated by it and loved it.

Mary Garber

During the war, women did everything. My college roommate joined the WASPs, the Women's Airforce Service Pilots, who flew planes during the war. She was the best brought up young lady in the world, but she wanted to do something.

When the war was over and the men came back, some of the ladies went back to other things, and there was a chance for me to cover high school sports. With high school sports, there wasn't as much of the what-are-you-doing-around-here attitude. They didn't care if a woman or a man or a monkey was covering their games.

When I moved into covering college sports in the early fifties, a lot of kids I'd covered in high school were in college, and I knew them. At the beginning, when I went to cover one of the colleges in the Atlantic Coast Conference, they wouldn't let me sit in the press box because women weren't allowed. And mind you, I was covering the game.

So they put me in the guest box with the wives of all the coaches. I was trying to cover the game play by play, and they were saying, "Now as soon as this game's over, you come by the house." And "John got up this morning in a bad humor and the kids were screaming and I thought I was going to kill them all." The little children in the box were jumping up and down, beating on the table and screaming at the team. I nearly went insane.

I came home and complained to the managing editor. He wrote a letter to the presidents of Duke, North Carolina State, Wake Forest, and the University of North Carolina —the four Atlantic Coast Conference schools in North Carolina. He said that it was up to the *Winston-Salem Jour-*

PART THREE

nal-Sentinel to decide which reporter it would send to cover a game and that it was not their business to discriminate against any staff member who was sent there. I am also told that he wrote that if the *Journal-Sentinel* wanted to send a monkey to cover the game, the monkey should be admitted to the press box! I won't vouch for the accuracy of that, but one of the men told me that. Anyhow, I never had any further trouble getting admitted to the press box.

An association was started for writers who covered the Atlantic Coast Conference, and I was barred from that: it was for men only. The paper pays the dues. We got a new sports editor, and he sent in the dues for me, not knowing I wasn't eligible. It got past the treasurer. He didn't know it either. There was a great flack when they realized what had happened. So the association had a hurried executive board meeting and finally decided to go ahead and let me be a member. The year before last, I was president of the organization.

Maybe it's like a bunch of boys having a little sister tagging along after them, and they keep telling her, "Go home to mama. Go home to mama." After a while, they realize she's not going to go. Then they realize she might be able to play right field if they put her out there. I think that's it more than anything else.

I was among the first women sportswriters. Another one named Jeane Hoffman worked out in Los Angeles. She and I met after we'd both been in the business some time. A great many papers had women who did specialty writing in sports. They might cover a women's golf tournament or do an article on skating or some other special sport. But I'm talking about being a regular member of the sports depart-

Mary Garber

ment, really covering a beat and not doing just feature stories or just women's sports.

The greatest thing in the world about sports, about sportswriting, is that there's such a wide, wide variety of people in it. Sports have taught me, more than anything else, that good people come in all sizes, all shapes, all colors, all nationalities. Sportswriting has taught me that you can't take people and put them into little pigeonholes. People are just so different, and everybody's unique. Each individual, no matter who, can teach you something you didn't know.

Some people think of athletes as dumb jocks and would never imagine a basketball player being interested in roses, for example. Willie Hodge, who played at Duke, was an authority on roses. He took botany as an elective. I just happened to find out that he was interested in this, and I asked him about it. He started talking about the cross-pollination of roses. Somebody had offered a large sum of money to anyone who could grow a completely black rose. Hodge started going through the genealogy and cross-pollination it would take to grow a black rose, and he lost me completely.

I think most people in sports love what they're doing. They enjoy doing it more than anything else. Most of the coaches or professional athletes or college atheletes just can't wait for the season to start, are sorry when it's over, and can't wait for it to start again. I think it's marvelous to be in a business where you wake up in the morning and say, "I can't wait to start doing what I'm supposed to be doing," instead of dragging your feet and thinking, "It's nine o'clock. If I can just live until five, I can go home."

I like to be talking to the athletes and the coaches. I like

PART THREE

to be covering a game. I like to be out on the field of practice, anything but sitting in the office writing headlines, or something like that. Maybe 80 to 85 percent of my work is out of the office. There are nine people in the sports department, and everyone has to take a turn working in the office, doing the routine things.

The greatest thrill, to me, has been the chance to cover international competition. I covered the Davis Cup tennis matches when the United States beat Rumania in Charlotte, North Carolina. There was something really thrilling about seeing the team come in with *U.S.A.* across their uniforms and hearing "The Star-Spangled Banner" played. And when the American player got ahead, it wasn't "Stan Smith leads forty-thirty," it was "The United States leads forty-thirty." It was just very, very exciting. Everything was so impressive and serious.

Then the army band started playing what we thought was the Rumanian national anthem. The captain of the Rumanian team acted like he'd been stung by a bee. I didn't know what had happened. He started jumping around and screaming, yelling, and carrying on. We found out that the anthem they were playing was the one that had been the national anthem when Rumania was a monarchy. The Rumanians thought that was an insult and that we'd done it on purpose. We had the worst time trying to calm them down.

There was a Rumanian newspaperman covering the match. He had been pulled off the United Nations beat to cover the Davis Cup. He and I were talking in the pressroom and he said to me, "What would you do if you were in Rumania and they played the wrong national anthem for the United States?" I didn't dare tell him that we would burst out laughing. We wouldn't care if they played "God Bless America" or "The Stars and Stripes Forever." I apologized to him and told him we didn't mean any harm, that we were just stupid. He said, "Oh, no. You were not stupid. It was just a mistake." So we went and had a beer together, and the hand of international friendship was stretched between the Americans and the Communists.

Years ago there was an international track meet in Durham, North Carolina. When an international track meet begins, all the teams come in, separated by nations: the United States team comes in to the stadium together, the Pan-African team comes in together, and the West Germans come in together. But when the meet is over, international friendship prevails. The athletes walk around the track all mixed up. They hold hands and swing their arms, and the band plays. By that time, everyone has swapped uniforms so you really can't tell who's on whose team.

As they were marching around the Duke stadium, a couple of kids, fascinated, dropped down out of the stands and stood on the sidelines, watching. One of the athletes reached out to one of the kids and brought him into the march. The man who was announcing the event was really on the ball. He said, "Okay, kids. All of you, come." There must have been two thousand kids who came out of those stands. They joined the march, and the athletes picked the little ones up and carried them on their shoulders. The tears were just running down my cheeks as I stood there and watched it. We talk about how countries can never get along and how there can never be peace in the world. Here it was for just a minute.

PART THREE

Once I was talking with a Russian tennis player who spoke English pretty well. She was telling me how she just hated to practice. She said, "I just do everything I can to get out of practicing." We were laughing and carrying on, and all of a sudden, she froze. I looked over my shoulder, and one of the women who was with the Russian team, what they called a chaperone, had pulled up a chair and sat down. That girl's whole personality changed. She'd been outgoing. We'd been sitting there laughing and talking. And as soon as she saw that woman, she froze. She was absolutely scared to death. I've never had to have anybody teach me the value of democracy since! I wouldn't have stopped talking if an American chaperone had come around.

I think the toughest thing for any woman sportswriter to handle is the dressing room. I think the new breed of women sportswriter is just going into the dressing room whether the guys are dressed or not. The Atlantic Coast Conference basketball coaches have made arrangements to help the women. They've worked out a system whereby the dressing rooms are open to both men and women for fifteen minutes, then closed to everyone. This gives me the chance to get into the dressing room without running into any naked players. But football is still a problem. It's up to each school whether to admit women to the dressing room. Since I'll probably be the only woman on the Atlantic Coast Conference football beat this year, I don't have much hope.

Last year I was covering a basketball game in Raleigh, North Carolina. It was University of Virginia against

Mary Garber

North Carolina State. What I usually do is ask the sports information director at these schools to get me a player after he's showered and dressed. Barney Cooke, the Virginia sports information director, came up from the dressing room and said, "The guys are all dressed. It's perfectly all right for you to come down."

So I did. We were sitting around talking with the players and other sportswriters. The players were discussing the strategy and why Virginia did certain things. They were explaining why they ran certain offenses and defenses. All this time I'd been reading those men's stories, where they'd been analyzing the strategy and what the players were doing. And I realized that they were getting their information from the dressing room and I wasn't.

Until then, I had kept thinking, "Gosh, I'm dumb. Why can't I recognize such-and-such a defense?" Or, "Why can't I see that they're doing so-and-so?" The other writers didn't recognize these things any more than I did. They were talking with the guys in the dressing room. I sounded so much smarter in my next story than I usually did! It's a tremendous, tremendous advantage to be able to go into the dressing room.

Sports are a lot more than, as one of our colleagues used to say, "Who beat the ball game." Everybody who reads the sports page already knows who won the game. What they want to know is the things they can't find out for themselves: how the players feel and what they're like and why certain things happen.

You have to have the same qualities to be a good sportswriter that you have to have to be any other kind of newspaper person. You have to be willing to work hard, and if

PART THREE

you're a nine-to-five person, you don't belong in sportswriting. I think you've got to have a natural curiosity and interest, and you've got to be willing to do your homework, so that when you go to talk with an athlete, you know something about what he's done and something about the sport you're writing about. If you get caught in a position where you just flat out don't know, you'd better tell the person you're interviewing right from the start. I don't think anybody's born with mental discipline or the ability to work hard. I think you have to develop that. You've got to have an interest in what you're doing, an interest in people, and an interest in sports. If you're bored with it, then the story's going to be boring.

The only regret I have is that it's almost over. I think I'm like an athlete: when I get to the point where I'm not making a contribution to the *Journal-Sentinel* sports department, then I hope I leave or get out before somebody has to tell me to. I'm not married. This has been my whole life ever since I've been doing it. Now a lot of women sportswriters are married, but I think being a wife and a sportswriter would have been tough in my day.

When I started in the newspaper business, I had the dreams that everyone has, that I was going to be a foreign correspondent. I was very much interested in economics. When I went to Hollins College in Roanoke, Virginia, I didn't take journalism. I tried to get as broad an education as possible, which I think young journalists ought to do. I took a lot of economics; I took art history; I took languages. Somewhere in the back of my mind I sort of pictured myself as a female version of Ernie Pyle, the foreign correspondent. You know—go to some foreign country, write glamourous stories, and win a whole lot of Pulitzer Prizes. But I just never did that.

At one time, like most young people, I wanted to reform the world and cure all the things that I thought were wrong, such as poverty and wars. I think that was part of why I wanted to get into journalism. As I've gotten older, I realize that's not quite as easy as I once thought it was. All problems are a lot more complicated than I once thought they were. Sports have taught me that.

CHAPTER 12

Judith Crist —
Drama and Film Critic

Judith Crist is a journalistic critic, applying her journalism training and experience to reviewing drama and film. A Louis Harris poll in 1970 found that she was regarded as the most influential film critic in the United States.

Crist is known for saying directly and even bluntly what she thinks about the play or film she's reviewing. She's able to do so despite pressures not to offend the entertainment advertisers whose fees represent important income to many publications and television programs. Instead of worrying about the advertisers, Crist keeps in mind the person who's considering spending several dollars to see the movie.

She saw movie after movie as a child growing up in New York City; this turned out to be valuable training. Admission then was ten cents before five o'clock. She worked as a general reporter for eighteen years, reviewing off-Broadway plays after hours for the last five, before she became a full-time critic. The reporting experience gave her broad, general knowledge about many things, another asset to her in her work as a critic.

Crist's first critical assignment from the New York Herald Tribune—*to review a play—was unforgettable for several reasons. One was that her husband stayed home with their ten-month-*

Judith Crist

old son. When she returned from the play, the baby was missing. After a few panicky moments, they saw that he'd crawled underneath a sofa and fallen asleep. That episode notwithstanding, her husband encourages her in her work and is proud of her accomplishments, and their son grew up to become a writer.

Crist says she looks back on her life as a series of movie cuts and describes the missing baby crisis as a "particularly brilliant sequence." She looks ahead in the same way she anticipates each new movie, with the feeling that something marvelous is about to happen.

There is something about this profession that does not disqualify you because of advancing age, male or female. Once you have adapted yourself to your profession and adopted a life-style that will work with it, there is no reason for you ever to give it up.

When I say you have to adapt your way of living, I mean that from the very beginning you must feel a passion about a career that not many people do, because you have to be constantly on call. Your time is not your own. You're not a nine-to-fiver. You will not be able to plan your life very carefully. You have to be ready to go uptown and investigate a garbage heap or to leave for Chicago in twenty minutes because a murderer's going to be put on an airplane. I've been lucky that I've been able to live that way because I have a husband who is perfectly willing, as a nine-to-five public relations man, to be married to a woman who initially worked from one in the afternoon to nine o'clock at night.

I got my start on a morning paper; I've worked for weeklies and biweeklies and an afternoon paper. I've

PART THREE

worked for a so-called small intellectual magazine, the *Saturday Review,* although it's bigger than other small ones. Now I'm working for monthlies, as well as for *TV Guide.* I've done local and network television. With lots of luck, I've been able to taste it all.

Movies were the chief mass medium when I was growing up. You see, nice girls with college educations went to the theater. Movies were considered a total waste of time. The flipover in today's society would be if you sat home and watched television game shows all the time. I think I became interested in movies basically because I had a "deprived" childhood. I spent part of my childhood in Montreal, where you were not allowed to go to movies until you were sixteen. We saw only a very few kiddie shows. Then, when we were in Toronto for a couple of years in the thirties, my brother and I went to the movies on Saturday afternoons. That's where I discovered Dr. Fu Manchu and all sorts of wonderful nonserialized films. There were innumerable trashy, wonderful movies.

We moved to New York, and at that time, you could get into the movies for ten cents before five o'clock, fifteen cents after. Ritzy downtown movies were a quarter, fifty cents later in the day. In New York, I really became addicted. There were double features, and my mother's change purse was sort of always lying there! I was supposed to be swimming at the Y, or studying in the library, or visiting friends, or out walking. And there I would be at the Tower or the Fleetwood or Loews or RKO, just wallowing, sitting through double features.

I think the most important thing that my parents gave me was the sense that there are possibilities. Never for one

Judith Crist

minute did I think that I would not have a career, married or not. It was doing something in the world's work that interested me. I thought that was what you were born for. My mother came from Russia, where she had been a revolutionary. Here she became a New York City librarian and supported my father, when he was a student, in the early years of their marriage. When her first child was born, she became a housewife—a socially active one, even founding a library in Montreal while we were there. But for her generation, when the kids were little, you mainly supervised the house. It was only after my brother and I were in college that she began doing some translating work. She regretted this delay, and I regretted it on her behalf. I didn't know what an interesting person she was until the last years of her life, and unfortunately, she died young.

So I talked about growing up to be a drama critic. In my heart, I really hoped that someday I would be a movie critic. The odds were so against it, but I did feel if I became attached to a publication, I could get to be a critic. I was prolific in writing even before I learned to type, whether it was stories or poems or essays. I wrote for all the literary publications in high school and college. That was why I always knew I would be a writer, because if you're not writing, you're not going to be a writer. You can't suddenly say, "As of Wednesday I'm going to be a writer." I think it has to be somewhere deep in your blood.

One hallmark of the professional writer, I believe, is that you fall in love with words at an early age. This is how I know that so many of my students are really not going to be writers, because they say, "Well, I've been thinking of writing a novel." Charming. How many chapters have you

PART THREE

written? Or if you want to make films, how many have you made? I know one highly successful filmmaker who made twelve films in high school. It can be done with an eight-millimeter home movie camera, for example.

After college, I did graduate work in eighteenth century English literature while holding a teaching fellowship and then serving as a civilian instructor of English with the air force. Next I went to the Graduate School of Journalism at Columbia University and, after graduation, got a job with the *New York Herald Tribune*. It took me only eighteen years to get to be a movie critic there!

In the meantime, I was a reporter. I was an editor. I traveled the world and followed celebrities. I covered the greats and the nothings and the lost kids and the crowned heads of Europe. Not a minute of it was lost. I threw myself into all the things that came my way, although I always knew in my heart that I wanted to write movie criticism.

I started at the *Herald Tribune* as the assistant to Dorothy Dunbar Bromley, the columnist. Dorothy came to edit what was known as the Woman's Sunday Activities Page, which was a solid page in the Sunday paper, adored by all suburbanites and little old ladies, who were the bulk of the readership of that page. It listed every garden club activity, every bird-watching club, every needlepoint club in the entire metropolitan area. Dorothy said, "These items are of interest to perhaps ten people apiece. This is absurd. What we are going to do is deal with features of social importance to all women."

And it was great. In fact, the men at the *Tribune* used to call it the Sunday Social Significance Page! All we really had to do was find a woman on whom we could peg every story that we wanted to do, whether it was prices, or the draft, or how things are in India or Guatemala, or whatever. That page, under her guidance, became so good that you could no longer tell it from the rest of the Sunday features. It was so good a woman's page that everybody read it. It was a self-defeating thing and disappeared, ultimately. But Dorothy Bromley had the courage to believe that women are intelligent.

My newswriting experience was a great asset when I started writing criticism. General assignment reporting enables you to know a lot, a surprising amount, about a great many things. You need that in criticism. The thing that depresses me about so much of film criticism today is that it's done by people who have gone from the college screening room to the professional screening room and have never seen life in between, let alone lived a little bit. And I think that's important.

Reporting also teaches you that you are the filter, and that you're dealing with the inevitable truth, whether it's the way you saw an event or the way you saw a film. I've always felt you have to be an egomaniac to be a critic, because at least while you're writing, you believe you're dispensing the truth. I had, frankly, no intention of remaining a general assignment reporter all my life. Many people are capable of doing that, but I found it ultimately a repetitious and limited form of work. You begin covering things over and over and over. Your first national convention is the one to cover. After that, you already know the story.

So I was able to say to my editors, "I would be happier in my reporting work if you would let me do off-Broadway reviewing. I think you should let me do it, not just to keep

PART THREE

me happy, but because I think I can do it better than the person who is doing it." I said that because one of my college teachers, a nice Southern lady, had once said, "He who hath a horn, and tooteth it not, will die untooted." And she was quite right. I asked, and I got.

Because I asked and had gotten, you can imagine how I felt the first time I was given a play to review. It was on a Saturday night, and Saturday was my day off. It was about the only concession the *Tribune* made to married ladies. It also came with seniority, and I'd been working there for eleven years. The play was *The Golden Six* by Maxwell Anderson, which was opening at a rather posh off-Broadway house called the York. My husband stayed home to baby-sit with our ten-month-old son because our baby nurse had the day off, and I went with a friend.

When I arrived at the theater, I discovered that every first-string critic was there. There I was, sitting in the small off-Broadway house, the only second-string critic. New York had about seven or eight newspapers then. I remember the other critics were very nice and very warm to me because they knew me as a reporter.

I saw the play and I hated it. *The Golden Six* was all about terrible Nero and awful Caligula and terrible Mommy. This was Maxwell Anderson and a cast of very good actors, but I did not think they were giving good performances. I just thought it was terrible. And I was so afraid of being the new kid on the block who says, "Oh, the emperor has no clothes." Even then, I knew you could make a better reputation by being negative, by being vicious and funny, than you could by being moderate or being devoted. I was

Judith Crist

terribly nervous about the piece, about taking on a great playwright.

When I turned to film, I had been reviewing plays for about five years, and I was confident about my reviews. I knew film very well, having been practically a lifelong movie-goer. In film, that's invaluable. No movie you ever see is a loss. That's true in any journalistic specialty. Anything you encounter in your field is an enrichment.

The first year I was reviewing movies, up came *Cleopatra*. It is hard to imagine the three-year build-up for that film. Heads had fallen. Careers had been ruined. It was *the* event. I hate to call it a *cultural* event, but it was *the* event. And I thought it was terrible. Again, I was in that position. I was very nervous.

I really worked on that review. It was a tough one. Because it was a forty-million-dollar movie, I had to go into great analytic detail. I did not know that was the review that was to make me famous, both because of the denunciations that followed and the reprisals and everything else. It was a big story, like covering a presidential candidate. Other critics who didn't think the movie was much better than I did, didn't dare say so. They thought of the wrong things—the advertising, the forty million dollars, the broken hearts, and the everything else, all of which are totally irrelevant to the person who is going to pay three dollars to see it.

I also wrote a review of a Warner Brothers movie called *Spencer's Mountain* that led Warner Brothers to bar me from their screenings and to withdraw their ads from the *Tribune*. Instead of moving me to another position as the previous *Tribune* ownership would have done, Jock Whitney and

PART THREE

Jim Bellows wrote an editorial that appeared in the *Herald Tribune*. It was picked up by the Associated Press and saturated the country.

The editorial said something to the effect that "Our critic may be wrong, but our critic right or wrong. How childish can you be, taking away privileges and advertising? Are you under the benighted notion that this is going to change our critic's mind or that we are going to punish our critic?" It was brilliant. It had never happened before in the history of newspaper criticism. From that point on, editors throughout the country began to look quite differently at their movie critics.

Movies are a sensitive field because they advertise seven days a week. It's not seasonal. There are movie ads every single day of a newspaper's life. Entertainment advertising is also very expensive, mainly because of the fly-by-nights in the old days. Road show men would come through town, buy ads, and never pay for them. So the ads were very expensive, and the money had to be on the line ahead of time unlike, say, department store ads. The stores stay there, and you know they will pay for their advertising. Advertising fees are the base of a newspaper's income. Newspapers can't survive on circulation alone.

Newspapers had long scorned criticism, mainly movie criticism, because it had been such a "lowbrow" field and was closely tied in with advertising. So they would frequently pawn it off on women. In my newspaper prime, most papers in the country had women critics. It was chauvinism that led to the development of women critics. Men were too busy covering the "important" things, like basketball and baseball! Men got the sports coverage, and

Judith Crist

women got the "cultural stuff," which was considered less important.

There's much discussion about who's qualified to review which films. Some kid wrote to me recently about a movie about teen-age romance that I had not liked and this child had. I love kids who write nasty letters! They *will* speak, and they should. This child said he thought a teenager should have reviewed that movie. I asked in return, "Do you think a gorilla should have reviewed *King Kong*?" It's experience that counts, a knowledge of people and things that qualifies a critic.

The biggest boost I have had during this whole age of rock is having a child growing up. Every day from four o'clock on for endless years, he would come home from school and on would go his hi-fi. But I learned about rock. Unlike the other theater critics, when we went to the opening of *Hair* or *Jesus Christ Superstar*, I didn't have to say, "I don't know anything about this music. I don't like it, and therefore . . ." My son was my bridge to much of the culture of the sixties and early seventies. That was invaluable.

Through the years I've pioneered in several aspects of journalism. As a *Herald Tribune* reporter, I covered many areas—finance, syndicated crime, sports news, even pornography hearings—that women had not covered as an everyday assignment. I was the first woman drama editor of a major metropolitan daily. There we developed the first culture, or lively arts, section that consolidated the coverage of the various media and set a pattern for newspaper sections across the country and also was the basis of *New*

PART THREE

York magazine, which in turn has changed the face of magazine publishing.

My most prominent pioneer job came when I became film and drama critic on NBC-TV's "Today Show." I was the first network movie critic, serving for ten years. I was championed by the then producer of the "Today Show," Al Morgan. He never required that I have a script, permitting me to talk spontaneously. He gave me full trust that I was not suddenly going to start mouthing obscenities or go off my rocker. I had the honesty to express my opinion. You shouldn't be a critic if you're not going to do that. But I always say, "Who am I if nobody gives me a voice?" I could be the most courageous person in Christendom, but if nobody publishes me or lets me in front of the microphone, then I'm nothing. You need an honest editor or publisher or producer to be an honest writer or TV critic.

What I really enjoy about my work is what I have always felt about life itself. I don't care how depressed I am, I would never commit suicide, for the simple reason that I am convinced that something absolutely wonderful is going to happen tomorrow, and I won't see it if I am not there. In journalism, you never know what the day will hold. I think that's what ties people so to newspapers. I am always expecting to see the greatest movie ever made. But the fact that the greatest movie ever made won't be made in my lifetime, or will ever be made in anybody's lifetime, is what keeps me going.

To this day, after all the thousands of movies that I have seen, when I go into a movie house and the lights go down, I always feel that something *marvelous* is going to happen. It so seldom does. But I think that's what being a human

Judith Crist

being is about, that feeling that something marvelous is about to happen.

CHAPTER 13

Celestine Sibley —
ATLANTA COLUMNIST AND REPORTER

Celestine Sibley began working on the Mobile *(Alabama)* Press Register *when she was a fifteen-year-old high school student living in rural Alabama. When she didn't understand something about city life, such as a dirty word she'd never heard before, the men on the paper told her to ask the society editor, an older woman who was as knowledgeable as she was refined. Getting help from an experienced journalist when it's needed has been important to many young reporters.*

Sibley began working for the Atlanta Constitution *in 1941 and has worked there ever since as a columnist and reporter. One of many awards she's received was for a column inspired by a question her young daughter asked her in a coffee shop one morning. Another honor was being asked twice to serve as a juror for the Pulitzer Prize newspaper awards, among the most prestigious awards in journalism.*

The Georgia House of Representatives, which Sibley covered for the Constitution *for more than twenty years, passed an unprecedented resolution praising "... her dedication, her enterprise, her accuracy, her fairness, her ear for the language and her savor and appreciation of it, her flair for capturing the essential, her flawless response to humor, and her absolute sense of taste." For a journalist, each of these qualities is well worth striving for, although few achieve them all.*

Celestine Sibley regards journalism as one of the highest callings. She believes in the importance of "letting people know what's going on in the world," not just about politics, but about how different people live.

I had a friend in high school, an older girl, who worked for the high school paper. One day she told me in the hall that she was going to see the principal. I thought she was in trouble! She said no, she was going to interview him about some city service to the school, a transportation service or something.

And I thought, *imagine*, going and sitting in the principal's office and discussing *his* business with him! I said, "How do you get this job?" She said that if you made A's or B's in your junior year, you could elect to take journalism or dramatic arts. So I elected to take journalism, got on the high school paper, and was hooked. I loved it. It was more than just being able to talk to the high school principal. You can talk to governors and Presidents and movie stars and murderers—all kinds of people.

I had a teacher in high school who was a Georgia woman, and she used to talk to me about writing and about newspapers. She thought the most satisfying thing you could do would be to write something that people would read and remember for a little while. I believe she was right. Maybe you're not William Shakespeare and you don't write anything totally memorable. But to write some-

Mary Garber, sportswriter for the *Winston-Salem* (North Carolina) *Journal-Sentinel*.

COOKIE SNYDER

Judith Crist, drama and film critic. Crist knows Emma Bugbee from their *New York Herald Tribune* days. Upon learning that Bugbee had turned ninety, Crist wrote her and got back a "chipper letter."

RICHARD AVEDON

Celestine Sibley, columnist and reporter for the *Atlanta Constitution*.

KDKA-TV Photo by Jim Stark

Marie Torre interviewing President Lyndon B. Johnson in 1964 in Pittsburgh, Pennsylvania. She also interviewed Hazel Garland on her popular television talk show, "Contact."

Helen Thomas, White House bureau chief for United Press International wire service.

PART THREE

thing that is read and remembered for a little while is pretty good.

When I was in high school in Mobile, Alabama, I started working on the *Mobile Press Register* on Saturdays and during the summer. There was a woman on our paper who at that time was a society editor. But she'd been an old-time police reporter in New Orleans at the time when it was bloody. She was my mentor. Because I was a kid, the men used to send me in to ask her things I didn't understand. I grew up in the country, and I didn't know any dirty words. City children take them for granted, but I didn't know any. Every now and then I would rock the newsroom by asking some innocent question. They'd fall flat on their faces and say, "Go ask Mrs. Durham." She was a polite Southern lady whose family was from Charleston. She was completely elegant and gentle and kind, and knew all the dirty words and everything!

Then all the boys on the paper rearranged their schedules so I could go to Spring Hill College, which was in those days a Jesuit school for boys, They took female day students during the depression, and I was one of those. I went a couple of years, and then I got married.

Then I worked in Pensacola, Florida, on the *News Journal*. My husband worked there, and they gave me a job. When he came to Atlanta to work for the Associated Press, I followed him and got a job on the *Atlanta Constitution*. That was in 1941. I covered general assignments, then left to have a baby. I came back in 1945 and have been here ever since.

I don't know anything else, of course, but it seems to me that this is the highest calling. I don't believe any other profession is important! I think being a doctor or a lawyer or a minister *may* be important, but second only to letting the people know. I think it's important that people be informed of what's going on in the world, and not just politically. That's important too, but it's also important to know what's happening to other people, what it's like in other areas of life. If you're comfortable and well-heeled, you may not know what it's like to be a poor black woman in a bad situation with a child down in Grady Hospital because the house burned down. It's important to know that, I think.

I'm on the news staff and write my column too. My column appears under my name, and it can be about anything. I can review a book or interview somebody or write a personal thing about a walk in the country in the morning. Nobody ever tells me what to write. I won an award with a column I wrote years ago about a little girl asking a blessing in a coffee shop. It's been widely reprinted, and the two thousand dollar award money came in mighty handy! I couldn't identify the child in it as my child because it would have been like "smart sayings of children" or something.

Here's the way it happened. One morning we were pushed for time. The children had school, and I had to hurry and get to work. We went to this coffee shop and were seated at the counter. The atmosphere was interesting. It was near a hospital, and a man had been up all night waiting for a baby. The counterman was listening to news of Vietnam on the radio. Everybody at the counter looked kind of tired and discouraged and worn.

The waffles came, and my child, who was little, said,

PART THREE

"Mama, do we ask the blessing?" The counterman turned down the radio and said, "Sure we do, sister." He glared at everybody up and down the counter until they bowed their heads. Well, you know all children say, "God is great. God is good. Let us thank him for this food," and the rest of it. Afterwards, when people at the counter raised their heads, it seemed to me that the atmosphere in the coffee shop had changed. People were friendlier, and they started talking to each other. And I wrote it like that.

The bronze medallion I won said, "It is better to light one candle than curse the darkness." I couldn't go to Hollywood to accept it because I couldn't afford to. But Loretta Young, the actress, accepted it for me. All the lights were off in my house at the time. We lived in an old house with faulty wiring, and I used the prize money to get my lights turned on!

I think writing a column is fun and interesting, and it's nice to have leeway to write anything you want to, but I think what's important is to cover the news. I covered the Georgia legislature for twenty years. I've covered the Democratic and Republican national conventions and Jimmy Carter's inauguration. I covered James Earl Ray's many trials in Memphis in connection with the killing of Dr. Martin Luther King, Jr. I covered Arthur Bremer's trial in Maryland after he shot George Wallace.

Awhile back, I had one of those crazy days you always remember. It threatened to be a right dull day. The city editor said that Lady Astor was in town. Nancy Astor had grown up in Virginia and had married a peer in England. She was a thorn in a lot of people's sides. She was an outspoken, forthright person who said exactly what she

Celestine Sibley

thought. She came to Savannah, for instance, and said that Savannah was like a beautiful lady with a dirty face. After that, they got the dirt and garbage in the city cleaned up.

Anyway, she was in town visiting somebody, and I was assigned to call her up and go out and see her. I called and asked if I could. She said, "My dear, I'm going out to play golf. You couldn't interview me if your name was William Shakespeare." So I wrote a story about that.

I covered another story the same day. At the time, the workers in a meat-packing house were on strike. A couple of young people who had met in the picket line were getting married, and I covered their wedding. They were married in the picket line, and they went to the Stockyard Café for their wedding reception. The jukebox was playing "She's Too Fat for Me." The girl *was* fat. It was just one of those unforgettable days.

I've written eleven books, and several of them have had stories about people I've met in the line of duty. It's the people you meet and the lessons you learn from them that are important. Usually they are poor, sometimes ignorant, often disreputable.

There was one old gal who had triplets and was being evicted from a slum. She and I became best friends. I think I learned from her kind of an acceptance of life and pleasure in it. Things never got so tough that she couldn't laugh. She always had boundless faith that things would be better tomorrow. I think of her often when things get rough for me. I think of her and how she had real trouble and how she always laughed. She'd call me and say lightly, "We're going to be set out on the street, and hit a-rainin'."

Years ago there was an old lady who sold papers down

PART THREE

here on the corner, Ms. Arizona Bell. She had been a circus rider in her day. She and I were good friends. The Metropolitan Opera used to be a big thing in Atlanta. It still comes, but they used to make a lot more of it than they do now. I asked Ms. Bell to go, and I dressed her up and took her for a story. She didn't mind. She said, "I was in show business once myself." I spent the day getting her ready, getting her to the beauty parlor, getting her an evening dress, flowers, a chauffeur, and a car. And I got her there. There're not too many fools and jackasses that I have contact with. I know they exist, but I don't run into many of them. The only snob I knew saw us taking pictures of Ms. Bell making her entrance. She rushed up and said, "Who's the celebrity?"

And I said, "I'll tell you later."

My snobbish friend said, "Get my picture with her!" So I was delighted to get the picture. She didn't know until later that the "celebrity" was an old newspaper seller.

Loving the work is the main thing. People who don't like it don't stick with it. My husband was an alcoholic and died when my children were young. Having three children to feed kept me working harder than I might otherwise have worked. It was sheer necessity. But I like my work. Things used to be rough at home and I would come to town on the bus and get off and start walking toward the newspaper building. I'd feel my spirits lifting. I had this feeling, "Anything can happen today." I was at home in this world and could manage, handle it. Sometimes you can't handle your personal life.

My children look back now on a very happy and rich

childhood. We always went to plays, concerts, and the ballet. We saw all the movies at screenings, and occasionally there'd be a movie star or somebody who became a friend. They got to know them, and they kind of felt in touch with life.

It's perfectly true that for a long time, women haven't been paid as much as men. When you're trying to raise a family, that gets discouraging. I guess that has always been a problem for women. I don't know that the opportunities haven't been equal. Maybe they haven't. It just happened that I didn't want an executive job. Once I had a chance to be a backup for a city editor, and I hated it. I'm sure there are some women who would like it, but I couldn't stand it. You get into a desk job and you're hamstrung. You don't write. You don't cover. And the best thing about newspapering is getting out and covering the story.

CHAPTER 14

Marie Torre —
Freedom of the Press

Marie Torre was probably the first woman to go to jail for refusing to reveal a news source. She could have avoided her jail sentence simply by naming the man who gave her information for one of her newspaper columns. But if she had given his name, the free flow of information that is needed between source and reporter probably would have been inhibited, for her and for other reporters throughout the country. Torre believed that the principle of press freedom, including the right to keep news sources confidential, was more important and chose to serve her ten-day sentence.

The night before she went to jail, a friend called her and warned, "Someday your son will be applying to college, and a questionnaire is going to ask if his parents were ever in prison." Torre replied that they'd just have to find another college. Her son, Adam, did go to college, and majored in communications. He told his mother that every now and then her case is mentioned in his texts.

Here Marie Torre describes her early training in journalism, giving credit to one outstanding high school teacher who had a great influence on her. She also tells about the persistence and ingenuity it took to get her first job, the events that led to her imprisonment, and what it was like to be in jail.

Marie Torre

I was very fortunate. I found out at sixteen that I wanted to be a journalist. Through no effort of mine, there was a system at my high school in Brooklyn whereby students with averages of eighty-five or more in English were automatically placed in journalism-English classes. They did this because not enough students were signing up for journalism. They forced the situation, you might say. Until then I had been concentrating on business education.

So I found myself in one of those classes. I wasn't very happy about it because the instructor had a terrible reputation for being an ogre. His first words to us were, "Anyone who doesn't want to be in my class, get out and get your class changed!" I think I would have made that change if I'd felt that once I got out I could have changed my class. But I thought, suppose I do move out and I can't get the class changed? It'll be terrible to live with him.

Instead, I just steeled myself and remained in my seat, which turned out to be one of the best decisions I've ever made. Dr. Anton B. Serota was a magnificent teacher. In fact, he was *the* teacher in my life. There should be at least one such teacher in everyone's school experience. Dr. Serota guided me, inspired and prodded me to explore my potential as a newsperson. He was the faculty adviser to the school newspaper, and he invited me to work on it. I became editor of it, eventually. Dr. Serota did not restrict us to reporting just on school matters. He encouraged us to seek interviews with journalists on the New York newspapers.

After graduation from high school, I prepared to try to find a copygirl summer job in New York City. My point was to find out if this was the kind of work I really wanted.

PART THREE

So I proceeded to go to all the newspapers in New York. But I never got beyond the receptionist's desk, which was very upsetting.

Why I was still looking in August, I don't know. It was so close to my freshman year at New York University. But I woke up one morning and decided, "I'm going to get a job today if I have to go to the editor's home." I walked to the *New York World-Telegram and Sun*. En route, I said to myself, "You've got to have a story to get past the receptionist." A friend of mine worked for *Who's Who in America*, so I made up this story that I was from *Who's Who in America* and that I was assigned to interview Lee B. Wood, who was the editor. I knew all the editors' names very well—I'd done my homework.

The receptionist at the *World-Telegram and Sun* was a male, who interestingly enough, later worked for me. I told him that I was from *Who's Who*. He said, "Oh, you have to have an appointment to see Mr. Wood."

I said, "Can I make one now?"

He said, "Well, just a minute." He called Mr. Wood's secretary. When he hung up the phone, he handed me a piece of paper. He said, "Write your questions on this, and we'll see that Mr. Wood answers them." Well, that would have meant that I would not see Mr. Wood, that I would send him my questions, he would dictate his answers to the secretary, and I'd never see him.

I said, "Oh, I'm sorry. I can't do that. We don't do business that way. I have to see him personally." The receptionist was a little annoyed at that. He called Mr. Wood's secretary again. When he hung up, he looked at me suspiciously.

"Hey," he said. "Are you by chance looking for a job?" I was startled that he'd guessed the truth.

"No, no, no," I said. "I have a job. I'm with *Who's Who in America.*"

He looked at me long and hard. "If you want to wait, Mr. Wood will see you." So I did.

Then I *really* became frightened. I thought, "Oh, when Mr. Wood finds out why I'm here!" I was so nervous, so frightened. Finally Mr. Wood's secretary appeared, and she ushered me into this office. It was a long walk, a hallway that was like the last mile!

As I entered Mr. Wood's office, he was concluding a meeting with his department heads about that day's first edition. He acknowledged my presence, beckoned, and suggested I sit down until he finished, which I did. Then, when he dismissed his department heads, he called me over.

At that point, my voice was pitched so high I could hardly talk. I said to him, "I have to confess to you now. I'm not from *Who's Who.* I'm looking for a copygirl job." He was not only surprised, but obviously speechless. Then he burst out laughing. He thought it was funny that a teenager could put something over on a big town newspaper editor. He was a big man, too, with a bulldog face and bald head. He was at least six feet four.

He looked over my scrapbook of clippings and my high school journalism medal and said, "To tell you the truth, we don't like to hire copygirls. We've had only one. We usually have boys. And anyway, there're no openings now. But I'll tell you what. You send me an application personally, and when there's an opening, I'll send for you."

PART THREE

I left Mr. Wood's office thinking, "I'll never hear from him." But I was so pleased with myself for having done that. In early November, I came home from classes at NYU one day and my mother said that the *World-Telegram* had called about a job. I quickly called back. They wanted me to work full-time, but I prevailed upon them to put me on part-time until the end of the semester, at which point I said I would switch to evening classes and work full-time. They agreed to do this.

I don't say that others should look for a job the way I did. But I do say they should not rely on the traditional methods of getting a job. Sometimes it's the unusual thing that gets the job. It's interesting how the important things happen in one's life. I still feel I got that job mainly because the man who was in charge of the copyboys and girls was Italian, and I'm Italian.

When the end of the semester came in December, I switched to evening classes and went to work full-time as the managing editor's secretary. The job was a sought-after one because all his secretaries became reporters. I worked there a year and a half.

Things were moving much too slowly for me, when finally I did see a little opening that would at least get me into the writing end of the business. The amusements department was being reorganized, and an assistant was needed for the amusements editor. This department covered the arts, music, theater, nightclubs, concerts, restaurants, radio, and television. The editor of the department was also a columnist. What he needed was an assistant who could do the makeup for the section after taking care of all the details. It was like running a small-town newspaper.

Marie Torre

There were news items to be written, pictures to be placed, and space to be allocated for the critics.

I asked for the job and got it. The editor was a very strange man. One time he disappeared. He turned up after a few days; then he disappeared again. He never turned up again. Very strange. I was accused of wanting his job very badly!

At first the executives let me do the work, but wouldn't give me the title or the pay increase. Lee B. Wood said I was too young for the job. But I could do the work. That was okay! By that time, I was almost twenty and so eager to do the job that I didn't really care about title or money. I was doing the work, and that was what was important to me. Some time later, I was given the title of amusements editor. I had many front-page stories, wrote a column twice a week, and did Saturday magazine pieces. I did lots of writing.

The reason I left was that I wanted to do a daily column, which I had been told I would have after a certain period. But it wasn't happening fast enough. None of these things ever happened fast enough for me. I wanted to leave the *World-Telegram* and work for the *New York Herald Tribune*. I called a man I knew there, a columnist. He said, "Gee, it's interesting that you're calling me. I've been thinking of you." The *Tribune* was about to publish a TV magazine, and he was to be editor of it. He said, "I don't see why you couldn't be associate editor." He was looking for someone to do most of the work!

It was a strange feeling, leaving the place where I started. I was secure there. But I also had drive, and the *Tribune* turned out to be professionally rewarding. I did a

PART THREE

lot of writing, reviewing, and five- and ten-part series—for syndication. My column also was syndicated.

Then in 1959 there was an incident that resulted in my going to jail. It had to do with a column I had written about Judy Garland, the singer and actress. It was actually a routine column about her first television special. I had heard there was a problem between Judy Garland and CBS, the network that was doing the special. So I called a source of mine at CBS, an executive and a good contact, and I said, "What about the special with Judy Garland? I hear there's a problem."

"Oh," he said, "Marie, as late as yesterday afternoon we were ready to call it quits. Here we are close to the time of this special. We've tossed half a dozen ideas at her for it. She's rejected each one, and hasn't come up with an idea of her own."

I said, "What do you think the problem is?"

He said, "I don't think she wants to work."

I kept pursuing that. "Why doesn't she want to work?"

And he said, "Oh, I don't know. Probably she thinks she's terribly fat," which she was at the time.

I quoted him verbatim. The day the column was published, I heard from Sid Luft, Garland's then husband and manager. I ran another column on his defense of her and forgot about the whole thing.

A couple of months later, my husband and I were sitting around the apartment reading the newspapers. My husband saw this story in the *Daily News* about a suit Judy Garland had filed against CBS for $1,393,333. It didn't mention me or the *Herald Tribune*, but it said the suit was based on a newspaper column, and that she was suing for libel

Marie Torre

and breach of contract. We recognized the quotes from the column. I was quite pregnant at the time with my first child.

The very day Adam was born, I had a call from my city editor saying that the *Tribune* lawyers wanted to talk to me because we were involved in the suit Judy Garland had filed against CBS. My first day back home from the hospital, the lawyers came to see me. They were very concerned because they said there could be real problems. I couldn't understand their pessimism. I said, "Well, look, gentlemen. If it's not a written law that newspaper reporters protect their sources of information, it's certainly an unwritten one. I can't imagine any judge in the land forcing a reporter to talk." They didn't quite go along with that.

I was taken before Judge Sylvester Ryan in Federal Court in downtown Manhattan. I was holding pat on my story, which was that I could not continue to write the kind of column I had been writing if I revealed my source, because my sources would dry up. He listened to both sides, and then he said, very *cordially,* "Oh, Miss Torre, I think that people will still talk to you." He said, "There's no law in the land that protects the reporter from revealing a source. You have to give the man's name!" It's true there was no such law in New York, although there is one in several other states.

It was shattering. By the time I left the judge's chambers, I was visibly upset—so much so that a *Herald Tribune* lawyer took me for a cup of coffee and said, "Why don't you call your source and tell him the predicament you're in?"

I said, "I can't do that. What do I tell him? Hey, for

PART THREE

giving me this information, I'm going to give your name?" He could have lost his job.

Back at the office, I had to write a column. I don't know how I was able to do it in my emotional state. What further troubled me was that I didn't know how the newspaper felt. Most of the time, newspapers don't want to take on problems, especially when they're going to involve expensive legal procedures.

By the time I finished the column, there was a call from Ogden Reid, the publisher. I went to his office, and he said he had been informed of what had happened in court that morning. He said, "It's your decision, Marie. Whatever you want to do is okay with me. I just want to say one thing to you. I think there's a very important principle involved here. I'll stand behind you if you do not want to reveal your source. I'll fight it for you all the way to the Supreme Court if necessary. If we lose, it may mean a day in jail." I breathed a lot easier at that point.

The judge had said I had to return the following Monday and give the source's name. When I did go back, it was in style, accompanied by the *Herald Tribune* crime reporter and a photographer. The sight of them made a difference in the judge. Suddenly he was warm and gracious. He even called me the Joan of Arc of my profession. He was talking in quotes at that point.

The judge paved the way for our appeal to the U.S. Appellate Court. After about ten or eleven months, the U.S. Appellate Court ruled that although forcing a reporter to talk could represent a curtailment of press freedom, the individual's right to fair trial was a more precious freedom, and therefore I was obliged to give the source's

Marie Torre

name. We then appealed to the U.S. Supreme Court. We didn't have to wait long for a decision. A brief announcement was issued to the effect that the court would not review the case, noting that Justice William O. Douglas was a dissenter, meaning he thought the issue was important enough to review. This meant returning to court, and of course, the jail sentence.

I went back before Judge Ryan. Now he was upset. He wasn't calling me the Joan of Arc of my profession. He suddenly was calling me a troublemaker of the worst sort. This reaction may have been prompted by the fact that he was getting a lot of adverse mail saying, "Why send someone like that to jail when all these crooks and criminals are out on the street?" So he said I was worse than those crooks. He compared me to the troublemakers who at that time were bombing synagogues in the South. He said I was worse because I was a member of the profession that molds public opinion. He said that I was to give the name of the source right then and there. My lawyer said that I was firm in my stand and that I would not give the name of my source.

Then the judge said, "Get the marshal," which was frightening to hear.

My lawyer stood up and said, "I had led Miss Torre to believe that she would have some time to prepare."

The judge said, "I see no reason to delay this any further. Get the marshal."

My lawyer said, "But she has two very young children." (Meanwhile, I'd had another child. Adam wasn't quite two, and Roma wasn't quite one.) So with that, he relented. He agreed to hold off a week. I was to appear the

PART THREE

following Monday to surrender to the court, as they put it. It was New Year's over that week. New Year's Day, 1959. I'll never forget it. It was terrible. The judge could have made his point and then suspended the sentence. I don't know why he didn't do that. Anyway, I prepared for jail. The night before I went was memorable. I had calls from many friends who were concerned. One of the most interesting calls came from a telephone operator at the *Herald Tribune.* I don't know anything about her background, but she revealed part of it to me. "Honey," she said. "Let me give you a word of advice. Take a comfortable pair of shoes." Obviously, she'd done time.

The next morning, I told my husband to make sure neither my mother nor father was around the apartment. I couldn't bear the emotional tug. I knew my mother would be dissolved in tears and so would I. It's a terrible feeling to leave your home to go to jail. The children were so young. Well, it came time, and I proceeded to kiss them good-bye. Before I got to the second one, I kissed my housekeeper. She started to cry, and that's all I needed. I started to cry, too, whereupon I just ran out of the house without kissing my second child.

Court is an awesome thing, even if you're not involved in a case. When you are involved, it's much worse. The courtroom was packed. Many newspaper people had come in silent sympathy, as they said. What made me feel even worse was that at some point during the courtroom procedure, I saw my father standing in the rear. There was standing room only. I thought, "Oh, God, what a terrible thing for him to see this happening."

The judge asked my lawyer if I'd changed my mind. He

Marie Torre

said, no. The marshal came to me with his assistant. They flanked me, and while everyone else remained seated in the courtroom, I was asked to rise and walk out of the courtroom. It's a terrible, terrible ritual.

There was a long walk. We had to go to the marshal's office to pick up some papers, and there was this endless walk down marble halls. Reporters and photographers were following us and clicking away, taking pictures. As I walked, the tears welled up in my eyes. It was getting worse and worse. When we approached the office, I ran in ahead of the others. I saw a couch and threw myself on it. I cried uncontrollably, which was just what I needed.

Once that was over, I said to myself, "Now, listen. Consider this an adventure. You may never have another opportunity to be in jail." I was okay. I was taken by car to the Hudson County Jail in Jersey City, New Jersey, and during the ride, I had a good laugh. A matron riding with us said, "My, there were more reporters and photographers here for you today than there were for Frank Costello." So now I was compared to a member of the underworld. The funny thing was that New Jersey at the time was one of twelve states with laws protecting news sources. In other words, what I had done was not a crime there.

Anyway, I went through the whole process. Mug shot. Fingerprints. They took everything from me, even my purse. My wedding ring. My make up. My mirror. They issued a striped uniform, believe it or not, and a white cotton slip. I was to sleep in the slip. We had no duties other than to mop the floor in the morning and to make up the beds. While we were doing that, one of the other inmates came around with a big kettle of coffee. They called it coffee

PART THREE

—it was like hot water. Then another one of the inmates came around with breakfast. It was an animal existence. There was no door on the toilet facilities, and some of the male guards would come around. It was just degrading.

There were three dormitories and a cell block. Most of the women were in the dormitories as I was. I was the only civil prisoner, so I was alone in the smallest dormitory. There were sixteen female inmates and more than two hundred males. The inmates were very interesting. The women's charges ran the gamut from prostitution and child abandonment to the most serious charge, which was first-degree murder: a woman had shot and killed her husband. Interestingly, she was the nicest one. A person with a first-degree murder charge seldom has a criminal mind. It's usually something that's done out of passion. In this case, the woman's husband had beaten her many times, and she had been sent to the hospital on several occasions with broken ribs and other injuries.

It was really pathetic. Every inmate had to tell me her story. Talk about soap operas! The one thing these women had in common was that, almost to a one, they had been on their own at an awfully early age. They came from broken homes, or homes where they had neither love nor attention. They really responded to any kindness. Every evening I would pass out candy, cookies, cigarettes—whatever visitors had brought me.

One of the women cried when I left. It was because someone had cared for them. It really saddened me. The men had a TV in their part, but the women did not. So when I left I arranged for some company to give them one. The women had this one miserable radio that blared out in the hallway. It was just awful, but it was an interesting experience.

My husband was behind me all the way. He felt I had done the only thing that was possible for me to do. He had a much rougher time than I did while I was in jail. People were calling our home at all hours of the night. Reporters were calling too because they were looking for fresh leads every day. They would call him and say something like, "We understand that your wife is going to be sent to jail again," all kinds of things to upset him.

About two years later, Judy Garland and CBS canceled their suits against one another. (CBS meanwhile had sued Judy Garland for breach of contract.) People say, "How vital is it whether Judy Garland does a show?" It isn't vital. Of course it isn't. But where do you find the ideal case? The issue was right there, even though it wasn't a hard news story. I think it's very important to have a free flow of communication between source and reporter. It serves as a check on corruption.

The man who was sheriff of Hudson County at the time I went to jail had been a newspaperman. He had helped New Jersey adopt its law protecting news sources. He told me, "In the fifteen years we've had the law, no case has come up to test it. If you had given the source's name, you would have jeopardized our statute." When you hear things like that, you feel lucky to have been, in a sense, chosen.

CHAPTER **15**

Helen Thomas —
WHITE HOUSE BUREAU CHIEF

Helen Thomas started work in Washington as a hostess in a restaurant and today serves as White House bureau chief for United Press International wire service, the first woman to hold that post.

Coverage of the White House has changed dramatically since she began reporting on it during John F. Kennedy's administration. Journalists now have less tendency to protect the President and ignore his mistakes. The changes since Emma Bugbee and Kathleen McLaughlin spent the night in the White House have been even more pronounced. Security around the President is tighter. Television journalism has arrived. There are more women journalists.

Helen Thomas moved to the capital city from Detroit in the midst of World War II. She soon landed a job as a copygirl at the Washington Daily News *and from there moved to a broadcasting job at United Press Radio. She was able to keep her job when the men returned from the war because no one else wanted her early morning hours.*

Thomas went on to achieve a string of journalistic firsts. In addition to being the first woman White House bureau chief for a wire service, she's the first woman president of the White House Correspondents Association, the first woman officer of the National

Helen Thomas

Press Club, the first woman to open and close a presidential news conference, and the first woman member of the Gridiron Club, a noted organization of journalists in Washington, D.C. She said that the Gridiron Club accepted her because "the pressure from the women's liberation movement was on the club, and a lot of the male members realized that the time had come to enter the twentieth century." She shares the concern of some of the other pioneering women journalists for women's rights. Thomas wrote in her book, Dateline: White House, "Discrimination against women at all work levels has been distressing to me. Throughout my career, I've tried to move forward in this male-oriented profession." What has kept her going, she says, is simply the ambition to be a good reporter.

I wrote a feature story for the high school paper, and it got printed. That was it. It wasn't just seeing my name in print. I liked the whole idea, the involvement. So I began working on the high school paper. Even then, we had the long hours and the pressure on deadline days. Despite all that, I knew this was the career for me. I thought, "This is a great life." I had a one-track mind, and I never deviated from that.

I don't think my parents knew what a driving force it was with me at that stage of the game. I think they liked the idea, though. There was certainly no discussion. They wanted us all to be prepared and have careers, that's for sure. They had immigrated here from Lebanon and had nine children.

I just wanted to be a good reporter. That was the end-all, be-all. I had no desire to be an editor or publisher or to go up the so-called ladder, wherever the hierarchy takes

PART THREE

you, because I just plain enjoyed being a newspaperwoman. I went to Wayne University, now Wayne State, in Detroit. They had no journalism course per se, but they had some newswriting classes. I majored in English and liberal arts and worked on the college paper for four years.

Then I went to Washington, and after biding my time, I got a job as a copygirl on the *Washington Daily News,* now defunct. I received the munificent sum of seventeen dollars and fifty cents a week. I was thrilled! I got that job by making the rounds of the newspapers, making a pest of myself, just becoming a familiar face to the editors. I did see an ad in the papers, so I guess I was one of many who applied.

Next I went to United Press Radio, where I worked about twelve years, having to be at work at five-thirty in the morning. I got my job during World War II, when they were drafting men, so there were vacancies for women. A lot of women got fired right after the war, but I had such an obscure job that I was able to keep it. Noboby wanted to come to work at five-thirty in the morning, certainly not young men who were drafted as buck privates and came back as colonels.

I started covering the whole town when I joined United Press in 1943. I came to the White House in January, 1961, the beginning of the Kennedy era. All the First Ladies have been interesting, to put it mildly—Jackie Kennedy, Lady Bird Johnson, Pat Nixon, Betty Ford, and Rosalynn Carter. All of them have had something to offer, I think. When I started covering the White House, I did everything. There was such a concentration on Jackie and the kids that a lot of my copy was on them. But I was still

Helen Thomas

covering JFK too. When you start out as third person on a staff at the White House, you don't get exactly the top stories. But I've been doing hard news all along.

I was in the first group of journalists to go to Communist China in 1972, after a twenty-year break in relations with the United States. I think the China trip—eight days—was like landing on the moon, where everything was a story. That was my greatest adventure in journalism, just covering everything I could see, hear, feel, smell. The editors wanted everything. I had never had a field day like that before.

One of my toughest assignments was covering Watergate from the White House, where everything was shut down. There was a blackout on information. It was like a deathwatch, and that was hard, psychologically. We felt for the country, and we worried about things. We're watchdogs here, and we had this sense of tremendous frustration, this sense of doom.

There's no such thing as an eight-hour day. I can't predict how long my day will be because I don't know what story's going to break. I came in at around seven-fifteen in the morning on Monday this week and worked until one o'clock Tuesday morning. This was for the Chinese vice-premier's visit. That's fairly typical of a day when there's a state visitor. When I'm covering a state visitor and the state dinner and entertainment, then doing the story for the overnight wire, I know I'll be working until one, two, or three in the morning. When I cover conventions, of course, I don't sleep for five days. But my typical day, if there is such a thing, is maybe seven in the morning until seven-thirty at night.

PART THREE

In this job, you're leaping onto moving helicopters. You're jumping into cars in motorcades as they're taking off. You'd be in the line of fire if anybody were to get hit, such as a President, because you have to stay very close to make sure what's happening. You have to have very good legs to keep running, and you need a lot of stamina.

You need to care enough to be a journalist. Money has to be the least of your objectives, because the jobs we have don't pay in any manner, shape, or form. I mean the salaries don't coincide at all with what you'd get in TV broadcasting or other related fields. In print journalism, the salary certainly is not up to par, but the other rewards are great. You're involved with the world. You learn things first. You're constantly learning because every day's an education. You really have some sense of being alive and being involved with what's happening to the country and our people.

A wire service reporter has to be faster than a newspaper reporter. Everything that we think is a story goes out on the wire right away. We don't have time to sit and ponder it. Maybe that's bad because we don't have the depth of a reporter who has all day to work on a story and has six o'clock deadline. Anything that breaks here at the White House is a story. Speed and brevity are important. We can't go on for three pages. And four hundred words is almost the top limit, unless it's the Second Coming.

Now we're in the age of the computer so we work a little differently. We still dictate on the telephone if we can't get a computer or couldn't get the story out fast enough on a computer. Normally we just file stories into the Washington office, and they go out on the main wire all

Helen Thomas

over the world. In any case, we have to think fast on our feet.

We have to work on everything as reporters. I think we're constantly learning, trying to improve. We're gaining background. I don't think anyone just automatically becomes a reporter, picks up a telephone, and dictates a fast bulletin on the biggest story in the country, and does not have trepidations and make many mistakes. I'm still learning, I hope. Journalism isn't something that you can really learn in college. You have to *do* it. So I would suggest that interested young people try to get involved in a newspaper while they're going to college—the college paper or some other paper where they're working on a daily basis—to see what the demands are.

It's a totally competitive job, and every day we get a report card. United Press International is in constant, unremitting competition with the Associated Press, for one thing, and with all reporters in Washington, for another. So we have regrets every day that we pick up a newspaper and see that someone else got a story we should have had. But I have no regrets as to my chosen career. None. I think I'm the luckiest person in the world. I'm a nosy person, and I really enjoy getting the news!

I'm sure a lot of people think I'm aggressive, but I think that's absolutely necessary in this profession. I'm sure a lot of people think I'm obnoxious. I get occasional non-fan mail, which says that I'm ill-mannered and rude to Presidents. I think one should be sassy to Presidents. I think they should be talked back to, because we don't have monarchs in this country. I think they deserve respect. I treat them with respect, and I treat the office with respect, but

PART THREE

I don't treat any President with any special awe. The *office* does evoke awe, and I have that, I believe, and great respect.

But I'm just a natural iconoclast. I've never been in awe of people per se, because they're all too human. I have only an awe of the magnitude and responsibility of the job. If we report falsely from the White House, we can affect the whole world. Maybe I'm dramatizing, but it's true. So we hope that we'll always have the facts. We hope people will tell us the truth.

I've been a feminist from the day I was born. I have experienced discrimination in a thousand ways. But any woman has, in any professional career. It's been tough slugging, and the battle isn't won yet. I would tell young people to fight for the Equal Rights Amendment because it's their lives and it's their future. Their parents pay for their college educations and get them prepared, and all of a sudden they're turned down for a job because of being female. This can happen to them, they'll find out. So they'd better start working now for a law that demands equality. It's for them, really. I hope they realize that.

Of course there's been discrimination against blacks, and others too. Everybody's moving ahead, but it's a long road yet. Well, I just handle it with sheer grit. You suffer it out and vow to break down the barrier. You shouldn't have to start on unequal footing with a colleague or competitor because you're a woman. I mean we're all citizens. We all pay taxes. We're equal under the law, yet we don't have equality, not when professions are allowed to discriminate against women, and do.

I've been helped by many people—my colleagues, and editors who have forgiven mistakes. I think I've had tremendous help, more than I can ever acknowledge. Any discouragements I've had stem from being a woman, people saying, "Why don't you go try something else?" When I wanted to break out of radio writing and get into something else, for example. Most people want you to get out of their hair and go bury yourself. But I think you should always stay the course, follow your own instincts and convictions, and believe in yourself. That's the main thing.

I believe you should try to find a field that you don't feel is work. I don't feel that I've really worked. I feel great joy when I go to my job. When I walk through those White House gates, I always get a special thrill. I feel a sense of exhilaration and look forward to things that are going to happen, hoping to be able to fulfill the responsibilities.

Index

Abrams, Norma, 48, 67-74; and FBI, 67-68, 71; German saboteurs, 67, 72-73; Jack Diamond story, 67, 70-71; Lindberg wedding, 69-70
Advice for young people interested in journalism, 54, 73, 78, 84, 102, 112, 128, 139-140, 168, 182, 185
Anderson, Marion, 35, 39
Anspacher, Carolyn, 93-102; and George Bernard Shaw, 101; and Prince Faisal, 100-101; battle with Governor Reagan, 97; birth of the UN, 100; on writing, 93, 102
Associated Press, 119, 121, 122, 124, 150, 158, 183
Atlanta Constitution, 154, 156, 158

Bugbee, Emma, 21-26, 44, 45, 78, 156, 178; and Amelia Earhart, 24; and Eleanor Roosevelt, 22, 24, 25, 34-35, 37, 38-42, 45, 46, 47, 51; and Equal Rights Amendment, 23-24; covers women's suffrage movement, 23, 24, 25; five-day work week, 21, 25; last story for *Tribune*, 25-26; stays at White House, 38-39, 178

CBS, 170, 171, 177
Chicago Tribune, 27, 29-30, 34, 36, 38, 85, 99, 116
Churchill, Winston, 78, 79
Cleveland Plain Dealer, 111, 116
Crist, Judith, 142-153, 156; battle with Warner Brothers, 149-150; first critical assignments, 147-150; on writing, 145-146, 147; pioneering aspects of work, 151-152

Discrimination against women (in journalism), 21, 24, 30, 33, 40, 56, 67, 68, 69, 73-74, 81-82, 83-84, 91, 97, 101-102, 109-110, 115-116, 121, 123, 131, 133-134, 143, 150-151, 163, 167, 179, 184
Ducas, Dorothy, 35, 37, 42-43, 46, 47, 49-51

Earhart, Amelia, 24
Equal Rights Amendment, 23-24, 184

Federal Bureau of Investigation, 67-68, 71
Five-day work week, 21, 25
Flash lead, 72, 73
Freedom of press, 149-150, 164, 170-177
Furman, Bess, 37, 43, 46, 51

187

INDEX

Gangsters (organized crime), 27, 29, 30-32, 68, 70, 71; Big Tim Murphy, 27, 31-32; Jack Diamond, 67, 70-71
Garber, Mary, 131-141, 156; greatest thrill in sportswriting, 136; lessons learned in sportswriting, 135, 141; qualification for sportwriter, 139-140; toughest assignment for woman sportswriter, 138
Garland, Hazel, 99, 103-118, 157; and Harry Belafonte, 112; becomes city editor, 113-116; becomes editor-in-chief, 117; begins at *Pittsburgh Courier*, 105-109; begins column, 108-109
Garland, Judy, 127, 170, 171, 177
Gilman, Mildred, 48, 52-66; as sob sister, 60-62, 63; begins writing, 54; covers Nazi Germany, 53, 64-66; first job on New York newspaper, 54-55; stunt reporting, 48, 52, 53, 56-60
Goering, Hermann, 53, 64, 65
Gridiron Club, 179

Journalistic critic, 142-153
Journalistic education, 29-31, 33, 97, 100, 102, 125, 147, 165, 183
Journalistic ethics, 30-31, 50-51

Kennedy, John F., 127, 178, 181
Kuhn, Irene Corbally, 73, 85-92, 99; as war correspondent, 88-91; first broadcast, 87; in China, 85, 86-91; radio shows after WW II, 91

League of Women Voters, 37-38
Life, 122, 124
Lindberg, Charles, 69-70, 71

McLaughlin, Kathleen, 27-33, 36-39, 44, 45, 78, 178; and Big Tim Murphy, 27, 31-32; and Eleanor Roosevelt, 34, 35, 36-39, 46, 47, 51; covers gangsters, 30; early interest in reporting, 28; only woman on *New York Times* staff, 32; stays at White House, 38-39, 178
Morris, Mary, 99, 119-128; advertising photographer, 125, 128; describes her job, 120; freelance photographer, 126-128; in

Index

Russia, 127; uniqueness as a photographer, 119, 122

NBC (radio), 88, 89, 90, 91; (tv), 152
National Council of Negro Women, 103
National Press Club, 178-179
National Women's Suffrage Association, 23
New York, 151-152
New York Daily News, 67, 68, 69, 70, 71, 72, 73, 74, 170
New York Herald Tribune, 21, 22, 25-26, 35, 39, 77, 78, 79, 142, 146, 148, 149-150, 151, 156, 169, 170, 171, 172, 174
New York Journal, 52, 55, 56, 59, 61, 62, 63, 80
New York Sun, 23
New York Times, 28, 32, 34, 38, 44, 45, 61, 111, 116, 123
New York World Telegram, 88, 166, 168, 169
New Yorker, 53, 63, 66, 124
Newsprint, 112-113
Newswomen's Club of New York, 27, 86
Nineteenth Amendment, 21

PM, 124-125
Personal life vs. career, 50, 62-63, 67, 70, 96, 140, 143, 162

Photojournalism, 119-128
Pittsburgh Courier, 103, 105, 106, 107, 108, 109, 110, 111, 112, 113
Press agent, 23
Prohibition, 57-58, 70

Radio journalism, 85, 87, 88-92
Robeson, Paul, 53
Robinson, Jackie, 107, 109
Roosevelt, Eleanor, 22, 25, 28, 34-51, 53, 66, 91, 103-104; and Amelia Earhart, 24; and her press group, 34-51; and Marian Anderson, 35, 39; innovations of, 34; League of Women Voters, 37-38; "My Day" (column), 34; visits Appalachia, 40-41; visits Puerto Rico, 35, 41, 43, 46, 49
Roosevelt, Franklin D., 21, 25, 34, 35, 36, 38-39, 40, 41-42, 50-51, 78, 79
Running story, 95, 96

St. Louis Post-Dispatch, 116
San Francisco Chronicle, 69, 93, 94, 96, 100
San Francisco Examiner, 96
Shaw, George Bernard, 101
Sibley, Celestine, 154-163; on importance of journalism,

189

INDEX

158-159; on writing a column, 159-160
Sob sister, 63; defined, 52, 60; Mildred Gilman as, 60-62
Sports journalism, 131-141
Stringer, 103, 107, 108
Sulzberger, Arthur Hays, 32

TV Guide, 144
Tabloids, 67
Thomas, Helen, 157, 178-185; in China, 181; feeling about White House, 185; journalistic firsts of, 178-179; relationship to the President, 183-184; typical hours, 181; Watergate as tough assignment, 181
Tomara, Sonia, 77-84, 97-98; in China, 81-83; in India, 78, 80-81
Torre, Marie, 157, 164-177; column on Judy Garland, 170-171; gets first job, 165-168; high school journalism class, 165; legal battle to protect sources, 170-174; time in jail, 175-177

United Nations, 25, 28, 100 136
United Press International, 157, 178, 180, 183

Washington (D.C.) Herald, 53, 66
Washington Post, 116
White House, 38, 40, 42, 50, 103, 107, 157, 178, 179, 180, 182, 184, 185
Winston-Salem (North Carolina) *Journal-Sentinel*, 131, 132, 133-134, 140, 156
Women's National Press Club, 38
Women's Suffrage Movement, 21, 23, 25
World War II, 28, 53, 63-66, 67, 72, 77-79, 85, 88-91

Index

Russia, 127; uniqueness as a photographer, 119, 122

NBC (radio), 88, 89, 90, 91; (tv), 152
National Council of Negro Women, 103
National Press Club, 178-179
National Women's Suffrage Association, 23
New York, 151-152
New York Daily News, 67, 68, 69, 70, 71, 72, 73, 74, 170
New York Herald Tribune, 21, 22, 25-26, 35, 39, 77, 78, 79, 142, 146, 148, 149-150, 151, 156, 169, 170, 171, 172, 174
New York Journal, 52, 55, 56, 59, 61, 62, 63, 80
New York Sun, 23
New York Times, 28, 32, 34, 38, 44, 45, 61, 111, 116, 123
New York World Telegram, 88, 166, 168, 169
New Yorker, 53, 63, 66, 124
Newsprint, 112-113
Newswomen's Club of New York, 27, 86
Nineteenth Amendment, 21

PM, 124-125
Personal life vs. career, 50, 62-63, 67, 70, 96, 140, 143, 162

Photojournalism, 119-128
Pittsburgh Courier, 103, 105, 106, 107, 108, 109, 110, 111, 112, 113
Press agent, 23
Prohibition, 57-58, 70

Radio journalism, 85, 87, 88-92
Robeson, Paul, 53
Robinson, Jackie, 107, 109
Roosevelt, Eleanor, 22, 25, 28, 34-51, 53, 66, 91, 103-104; and Amelia Earhart, 24; and her press group, 34-51; and Marian Anderson, 35, 39; innovations of, 34; League of Women Voters, 37-38; "My Day" (column), 34; visits Appalachia, 40-41; visits Puerto Rico, 35, 41, 43, 46, 49
Roosevelt, Franklin D., 21, 25, 34, 35, 36, 38-39, 40, 41-42, 50-51, 78, 79
Running story, 95, 96

St. Louis Post-Dispatch, 116
San Francisco Chronicle, 69, 93, 94, 96, 100
San Francisco Examiner, 96
Shaw, George Bernard, 101
Sibley, Celestine, 154-163; on importance of journalism,

189

INDEX

158-159; on writing a column, 159-160
Sob sister, 63; defined, 52, 60; Mildred Gilman as, 60-62
Sports journalism, 131-141
Stringer, 103, 107, 108
Sulzberger, Arthur Hays, 32

TV Guide, 144
Tabloids, 67
Thomas, Helen, 157, 178-185; in China, 181; feeling about White House, 185; journalistic firsts of, 178-179; relationship to the President, 183-184; typical hours, 181; Watergate as tough assignment, 181
Tomara, Sonia, 77-84, 97-98; in China, 81-83; in India, 78, 80-81
Torre, Marie, 157, 164-177; column on Judy Garland, 170-171; gets first job, 165-168; high school journalism class, 165; legal battle to protect sources, 170-174; time in jail, 175-177

United Nations, 25, 28, 100 136
United Press International, 157, 178, 180, 183

Washington (D.C.) *Herald*, 53, 66
Washington Post, 116
White House, 38, 40, 42, 50, 103, 107, 157, 178, 179, 180, 182, 184, 185
Winston-Salem (North Carolina) *Journal-Sentinel*, 131, 132, 133-134, 140, 156
Women's National Press Club, 38
Women's Suffrage Movement, 21, 23, 25
World War II, 28, 53, 63-66, 67, 72, 77-79, 85, 88-91

About the Author

Jean E. Collins, who was born in Brunswick, Georgia, was a *Mademoiselle* guest editor and has worked as a newspaper and magazine reporter. She was graduated from Northwestern University and the Columbia University Graduate School of Journalism. She lives with her husband and daughter in Ellicott City, Maryland. This is her first book.